Integrated Chinese

Integrated Chinese

中文听说读写

Simplified Character Edition

WORKBOOK

2nd Edition

Tao-chung Yao and Yuehua Liu

**Yea-fen Chen, Liangyan Ge,
Nyan-Ping Bi & Xiaojun Wang**

CHENG & TSUI COMPANY ▲ BOSTON

10 09 08 07   10 9 8 7 6 5 4 3 2

Published by
Cheng & Tsui Company, Inc.
25 West Street
Boston, MA 02111-1213 USA
Fax (617) 426-3669
www.cheng-tsui.com
"Bringing Asia to the World"™

Integrated Chinese Level 1 Part 1 Workbook
Simplified Character Edition
ISBN 0-88727-462-5
ISBN-13 978-0-88727-462-6

The *Integrated Chinese* series includes books, workbooks, character workbooks, audio products, multimedia products, teacher's resources, and more. Visit **www.cheng-tsui.com** for more information on the other components of *Integrated Chinese*.

Printed in Canada

THE INTEGRATED CHINESE SERIES

The *Integrated Chinese* series is a two-year course that includes textbooks, workbooks, character workbooks, audio CDs, CD-ROMs, DVDs and teacher's resources.

Textbooks introduce Chinese language and culture through a series of dialogues and narratives, with culture notes, language use and grammar explanations, and exercises.

Workbooks follow the format of the textbooks and contain a wide range of integrated activities that teach the four language skills of listening, speaking, reading and writing.

Character Workbooks help students learn Chinese characters in their correct stroke order. Special emphasis is placed on the radicals that are frequently used to compose Chinese characters.

Audio CDs include the narratives, dialogues and vocabulary presented in the textbooks, as well as pronunciation and listening exercises that correspond to the workbooks.

Teacher's Resources contain helpful guidance and additional activities online.

Multimedia CD-ROMs are divided into sections of listening, speaking, reading and writing, and feature a variety of supplemental interactive games and activities for students to test their skills and get instant feedback.

Workbook DVD shows listening comprehension dialogues from the Level 1 Part 1 Workbook, presented in contemporary settings in color video format.

PUBLISHER'S NOTE

When *Integrated Chinese* was first published in 1997, it set a new standard with its focus on the development and integration of the four language skills (listening, speaking, reading, and writing). Today, to further enrich the learning experience of the many users of *Integrated Chinese* worldwide, the Cheng & Tsui Company is pleased to offer the revised, updated and expanded second edition of *Integrated Chinese*. We would like to thank the many teachers and students who, by offering their valuable insights and suggestions, have helped *Integrated Chinese* evolve and keep pace with the many positive changes in the field of Chinese language instruction. *Integrated Chinese* continues to offer comprehensive language instruction, with many new features.

The Cheng & Tsui Asian Language Series is designed to publish and widely distribute quality language learning materials created by leading instructors from around the world. We welcome readers' comments and suggestions concerning the publications in this series. Please send feedback to our Editorial Department (e-mail: **editor@cheng-tsui.com**), or contact the following members of our Editorial Board.

CONTENTS

Preface xv

Introduction: Pronunciation Exercises   1

Part One 1

  I. Single Words 1

  II. Tone Combination Exercise 5

Part Two 6

  I. Initials and Simple Finals 6

  II. Tones 6

  III. Compound Finals 7

  IV. Neutral Tones 7

  V. Exercises for Initials, Finals, and Tones: Monosyllabic Words . . 8

  VI. Exercises for Initials, Finals, and Tones: Bisyllabic Words . . . 8

  VII. Exercises for Initials, Finals, and Tones: Cities 9

  VIII. Exercises for Initials, Finals, and Tones: Celebrities 9

  IX. Exercises for Initials, Finals, and Tones: Countries 10

  X. Exercises for Initials, Finals, and Tones: American Presidents . 10

Lesson 1: Greetings   11

Part One 11

  I. Listening Comprehension 11

  II. Speaking Exercises 12

  III. Reading Comprehension 13

  IV. Writing & Grammar Exercises 13

Part Two 15

  I. Listening Comprehension 15

  II. Speaking Exercises 15

  III. Reading Comprehension 16

  IV. Writing & Grammar Exercises 18

▼▼

Lesson 2: Family — 23

Part One 23

    I. Listening Comprehension 23

    II. Speaking Exercises 23

    III. Reading Comprehension 24

    IV. Writing & Grammar Exercises 25

Part Two 27

    I. Listening Comprehension 27

    II. Speaking Exercises 29

    III. Reading Comprehension 29

    IV. Writing & Grammar Exercises 32

Lesson 3: Dates and Time — 37

Part One 37

    I. Listening Comprehension 37

    II. Speaking Exercises 38

    III. Reading Comprehension 38

    IV. Writing & Grammar Exercises 40

Part Two 43

    I. Listening Comprehension 43

    II. Speaking Exercises 44

    III. Reading Comprehension 44

    IV. Writing & Grammar Exercises 46

Lesson 4: Hobbies — 50

Part One 50

    I. Listening Comprehension 50

    II. Speaking Exercises 51

    III. Reading Comprehension 52

    IV. Writing & Grammar Exercises 54

▼ ▼

Part Two **56**

   I. Listening Comprehension 56

   II. Speaking Exercises 57

   III. Reading Comprehension 58

   IV. Writing & Grammar Exercises 60

Lesson 5: Visiting Friends   63

Part One **63**

   I. Listening Comprehension 63

   II. Speaking Exercises 64

   III. Reading Comprehension 65

   IV. Writing & Grammar Exercises 66

Part Two **69**

   I. Listening Comprehension 69

   II. Speaking Exercises 70

   III. Reading Comprehension 71

   IV. Writing & Grammar Exercises 73

Lesson 6: Making Appointments   77

Part One **77**

   I. Listening Comprehension 77

   II. Speaking Exercises 78

   III. Reading Comprehension 79

   IV. Writing & Grammar Exercises 83

Part Two **86**

   I. Listening Comprehension 86

   II. Speaking Exercises 87

   III. Reading Comprehension 88

   IV. Writing & Grammar Exercises 92

Lesson 7: Studying Chinese 97

Part One **97**

   I. Listening Comprehension 97

   II. Speaking Exercises 98

   III. Reading Comprehension 99

   IV. Writing & Grammar Exercises 101

Part Two **105**

   I. Listening Comprehension 105

   II. Speaking Exercises 105

   III. Reading Comprehension 106

   IV. Writing & Grammar Exercises 108

Lesson 8: School Life 111

Part One **111**

   I. Listening Comprehension 111

   II. Speaking Exercises 112

   III. Reading Comprehension 113

   IV. Writing & Grammar Exercises 116

Part Two **120**

   I. Listening Comprehension 120

   II. Speaking Exercises 120

   III. Reading Comprehension 121

   IV. Writing & Grammar Exercises 123

Lesson 9: Shopping 127

Part One **127**

   I. Listening Comprehension 127

   II. Speaking Exercises 128

   III. Reading Comprehension 128

   IV. Writing & Grammar Exercises 130

▼▼▼▼▼▼▼▼▼▼▼▼▼▼▼▼▼▼▼▼▼▼▼▼▼▼▼▼▼▼▼▼▼▼▼▼▼

Part Two 133

    I. Listening Comprehension. 133

    II. Speaking Exercises 133

    III. Reading Comprehension 134

    IV. Writing & Grammar Exercises. 136

Lesson 10: Talking about the Weather 141

Part One 141

    I. Listening Comprehension. 141

    II. Speaking Exercises 142

    III. Reading Comprehension 142

    IV. Writing & Grammar Exercises. 144

Part Two 147

    I. Listening Comprehension. 147

    II. Speaking Exercises 147

    III. Reading Comprehension 148

    IV. Writing & Grammar Exercises. 151

Lesson 11: Transportation 157

Part One 157

    I. Listening Comprehension. 157

    II. Speaking Exercises 157

    III. Reading Comprehension 158

    IV. Writing & Grammar Exercises. 160

Part Two 165

    I. Listening Comprehension. 165

    II. Speaking Exercises 165

    III. Reading Comprehension 166

    IV. Writing & Grammar Exercises. 170

PREFACE

In designing the Level One workbook exercises for *Integrated Chinese*, we strove to give equal emphasis to the students' listening, speaking, reading and writing skills. There are different difficulty levels in order to provide variety and flexibility to suit different curriculum needs. Teachers should assign the exercises at their discretion; they should not feel pressured into using all of them and should feel free to use them out of sequence, if appropriate. Moreover, teachers can complement this workbook with their own exercises.

The exercises in each lesson are divided into two parts. The exercises in Part One are for the first dialogue and those in Part Two are for the second dialogue. This way, the two dialogues in each lesson can be taught separately. The teacher can use the first two or three days to teach the first dialogue and ask the students to do all the exercises in Part One, then go on to teach the second dialogue. The teacher can also give the two separate vocabulary tests for the two dialogues so as to reduce the pressure of memorizing too many new words at the same time.

Listening Comprehension

All too often listening comprehension is sacrificed in a formal classroom setting because of time constraints. Students tend to focus their time and energy on the mastery of a few grammar points. This workbook tries to remedy this imbalance by including a substantial number of listening comprehension exercises. There are two categories of listening exercises; both can be done on the students' own time or in the classroom. In either case, it is important to have the instructor review the students' answers for accuracy.

The first category of listening exercises, which is at the beginning of this section, is based on the text of each lesson. For the exercises to be meaningful, students should *first* study the vocabulary list, and *then* listen to the recordings *before* attempting to read the texts. The questions are provided to help students' aural understanding of the texts and to test their reading comprehension.

The second category of listening exercises consists of an audio CD recording of two or more mini-dialogues or narratives. These exercises are designed to give students extra practice on the vocabulary and grammar points introduced in the lesson. Some of the exercises, especially ones that ask students to choose among several possible answers, are significantly more difficult than others. These exercises should be assigned towards the end of the lesson, when the students have become familiar with the content of the lesson.

Speaking Exercises

Here, too, there are two types of exercises. They are designed for different levels of proficiency within each lesson and should be assigned at the appropriate time.

To help students apply their newly-acquired vocabulary and grammatical understanding to meaningful communication, we first ask them questions related to the dialogues and narratives, and then ask them questions related to their own lives. These questions require a one- or two-sentence answer. By stringing together short questions and answers, students can construct their own mini-dialogues, practice in pairs or take turns asking or answering questions.

Once they have gained some confidence, students can progress to the more difficult questions, where they are invited to express opinions on a number of topics. Typically, these questions are abstract, so they gradually teach students to express their opinions in longer conversations. As the school year progresses, these types of questions should take up more class discussion time. Because this second type of speaking exercise is quite challenging, it should be attempted only *after* students are well grounded in the grammar and vocabulary of a particular lesson. Usually, this occurs *not immediately* after students have completed the first part of the speaking exercises.

Reading Comprehension

For the first seven lessons, the reading exercises appear in several different formats, including matching, translations, answering questions in English or answering multiple choice questions based on reading texts. There are also some authentic materials and modified authentic materials. Starting with Lesson 8, the format for reading exercises is fixed. The first section of the lesson asks questions based on the dialogues in the textbook. The second section offers several reading passages with questions that are relevant to the themes of the current lesson.

Writing and Grammar Exercises

Grammar and Usage

These drills and exercises are designed to solidify students' grasp of important grammar points. Through brief exchanges, students answer questions using specific grammatical forms, or are given sentences to complete. Because they must provide context for these exercises, students cannot treat them as simple mechanical repetition drills.

In the last three lessons, students are introduced to increasingly sophisticated and abstract vocabulary. Corresponding exercises help them to grasp the nuances of new words. For example, synonyms are a source of great difficulty, so exercises are provided to help students distinguish between them.

Translation

Translation has been a tool for language teaching throughout the ages, and positive student feedback confirms our belief that it continues to play an important role. The exercises we have devised serve to reinforce two primary areas: one, to get students to apply specific grammatical structures; and two, to allow students to build their ever-increasing vocabulary. Ultimately, our hope is that this dual-pronged approach will enable students to understand that it takes more than just literal translation to convey an idea in a foreign language.

Writing Practice

This is the culmination of the written exercises, and it is where students learn to express themselves in writing. Many of the topics overlap with those used in oral practice. We expect that students will find it easier to put in writing what they have already learned to express orally.

Introduction

Pronunciation Exercises

PART ONE

I. Single Words

Listen carefully and circle the correct answer.

A. Initials

1.a. pà	b. bà
2.a. pí	b. bí
3.a. nán	b. mán
4.a. fú	b. hú
5.a. tīng	b. dīng
6.a. tǒng	b. dǒng
7.a. nán	b. lán
8.a. niàn	b. liàn
9.a. gàn	b. kàn
10.a. kuì	b. huì
11.a. kǎi	b. hǎi
12.a. kuā	b. huā
13.a. jiān	b. qiān
14.a. yú	b. qú
15.a. xiāng	b. shāng
16.a. chú	b. rú
17.a. zhá	b. zá
18.a. zì	b. cì
19.a. sè	b. shè
20.a. sè	b. cè
21.a. zhǒng	b. jiǒng
22.a. shēn	b. sēn
23.a. rù	b. lù

B. Finals

1.a. tuō   b. tōu

2.a. guǒ   b. gǒu

3.a. duò   b. dòu

4.a. diū   b. dōu

5.a. liú   b. lóu

6.a. yǒu   b. yǔ

7.a. nǔ   b. nǚ

8.a. lú   b. lǘ

9.a. yuán   b. yán

10.a. píng   b. pín

11.a. làn   b. luàn

12.a. huán   b. hán

13.a. fèng   b. fèn

14.a. bèng   b. bèn

15.a. lún   b. léng

16.a. bīn   b. bīng

17.a. kěn   b. kǔn

18.a. héng   b. hóng

19.a. téng   b. tóng

20.a. kēng   b. kōng

21.a. pàn   b. pàng

22.a. fǎn   b. fǎng

23.a. dǎn   b. dǎng

24.a. mín   b. míng

25.a. pēn   b. pān

26.a. rén   b. rán

27.a. mán   b. mén

C. Tones: First and Fourth (Level and Falling)

1.a. pō   b. pò

2.a. pān   b. pàn

3.a. wù   b. wū

▼ ▼

4.a. tà	b. tā
5.a. qū	b. qù
6.a. sì	b. sī
7.a. fēi	b. fèi
8.a. duì	b. duī
9.a. xià	b. xiā
10.a. yā	b. yà

D. Tones: Second and Third (Rising and Low)

1.a. mǎi	b. mái
2.a. fǎng	b. fáng
3.a. dá	b. dǎ
4.a. tú	b. tǔ
5.a. nǐ	b. ní
6.a. wú	b. wǔ
7.a. bǎ	b. bá
8.a. shí	b. shǐ
9.a. huǐ	b. huí
10.a. féi	b. fěi
11.a. mǎ	b. má
12.a. dí	b. dǐ
13.a. láo	b. lǎo
14.a. gé	b. gě
15.a. zhǐ	b. zhí

E. Tones: All Four Tones

1.a. bà	b. bā
2.a. pí	b. pì
3.a. méi	b. měi
4.a. wēn	b. wěn
5.a. zǎo	b. zāo
6.a. yōu	b. yóu
7.a. guāng	b. guǎng
8.a. zhuāng	b. zhuàng

9. a. qì   b. qí

10. a. mào   b. máo

11. a. bǔ   b. bù

12. a. kuàng   b. kuāng

13. a. jú   b. jǔ

14. a. qiáng   b. qiāng

15. a. xián   b. xiān

16. a. yǒng   b. yòng

17. a. zú   b. zū

18. a. cí   b. cǐ

19. a. suī   b. suí

20. a. zhèng   b. zhēng

21. a. chòu   b. chóu

22. a. shuāi   b. shuài

23. a. wǒ   b. wò

24. a. yào   b. yáo

25. a. huī   b. huì

26. a. rú   b. rù

27. a. rén   b. rèn

F. Comprehensive Exercise

1. a. jiā   b. zhā

2. a. chuí   b. qué

3. a. chǎng   b. qiǎng

4. a. xū   b. shū

5. a. shuǐ   b. xuě

6. a. zǎo   b. zhǎo

7. a. zǎo   b. cǎo

8. a. sōu   b. shōu

9. a. tōu   b. tuō

10. a. dǒu   b. duǒ

11. a. duǒ   b. zuǒ

12. a. mǎi   b. měi

13.a. shào   b. xiào

14.a. chóu   b. qiú

15.a. yuè   b. yè

16.a. jiǔ   b. zhǒu

17.a. nǔ   b. nǚ

18.a. zhú   b. jú

19.a. jì   b. zì

20.a. liè   b. lüè

21.a. jīn   b. zhēn

22.a. xiǔ   b. shǒu

23.a. kǔn   b. hěn

24.a. shǎo   b. xiǎo

25.a. zhǎng   b. jiǎng

26.a. qū   b. chū

II. Tone Combination Exercise

You will hear one word at a time. Write down the tones in the blank. Use 1-4 for the four tones, and 5 for neutral tones.

Example: If you hear the word "Zhōngwén," you will write "1, 2" in the blank.

A.

1._____	11._____	21._____
2._____	12._____	22._____
3._____	13._____	23._____
4._____	14._____	24._____
5._____	15._____	25._____
6._____	16._____	26._____
7._____	17._____	27._____
8._____	18._____	28._____
9._____	19._____	29._____
10._____	20._____	30._____

B.

1._____	10._____	19._____	28._____
2._____	11._____	20._____	29._____
3._____	12._____	21._____	30._____
4._____	13._____	22._____	
5._____	14._____	23._____	
6._____	15._____	24._____	
7._____	16._____	25._____	
8._____	17._____	26._____	
9._____	18._____	27._____	

PART TWO

I. Initials and Simple Finals

Fill in the blanks with appropriate initials or simple finals.

A.1. __a	A.2. p__	A.3. __u	A.4. l__
B.1. f__	B.2. n__	B.3. __i	B.4. __u
C.1. __a	C.2. l__	C.3. l__	C.4. __u
D.1. __u	D.2. t__	D.3. n__	D.4. n__
E.1. __e	E.2. __u	E.3. __a	
F.1. g__	F.2. k__	F.3. h__	
G.1. __u	G.2. __i	G.3. __u	
H.1. j__	H.2. q__	H.3. x__	
I.1. __a	I.2. __e	I.3. __i	I.4. __u
J.1. __u	J.2. c__	J.3. __u	J.4. __i
K.1. __i	K.2. s__	K.3. __a	K.4. q__
L.1. __a	L.2. __i	L.3. s__	L.4. __u
M.1. c__	M.2. __i	M.3. __u	M.4. __a
N.1. __u	N.2. r__	N.3. ch__	N.4. __e

II. Tones

Listen to the CD and mark the correct tone marks.

A.1. he	A.2. ma	A.3. pa	A.4. di
B.1. nü	B.2. re	B.3. chi	B.4. zhu
C.1. mo	C.2. qu	C.3. ca	C.4. si
D.1. tu	D.2. fo	D.3. ze	D.4. ju

E.1. lü   E.2. bu   E.3. xi   E.4. shi

F.1. gu   F.2. se   F.3. ci   F.4. ku

G.1. mang   G.2. quan   G.3. yuan   G.4. yue

H.1. yi   H.2. er   H.3. san   H.4. si

I.1. ba   I.2. qi   I.3. liu   I.4. wu

J.1. jiu   J.2. shi   J.3. tian   J.4. jin

K.1. mu   K.2. shui   K.3. huo   K.4. ren

L.1. yu   L.2. zhuang   L.3. qun   L.4. zhong

III. Compound Finals

A. Fill in the blanks with compound finals.

1.a. zh____   1.b. t____   1.c. k____   1.d. j____

2.a. x____   2.b. q____   2.c. j____   2.d. d____

3.a. x____   3.b. zh____   3.c. t____   3.d. g____

4.a. sh____   4.b. b____   4.c. z____   4.d. q____

5.a. j____   5.b. d____   5.c. x____   5.d. ch____

6.a. zh____   6.b. l____   6.c. k____   6.d. j____

7.a. s____   7.b. x____   7.c. p____   7.d. ch____

B. Fill in the blanks with compound finals and mark appropriate tone marks.

1.a. m____   1.b. zh____   1.c. sh____   1.d. zh____

2.a sh____   2.b. t____   2.c. l____   2.d. b____

3.a. s____   3.b. j____   3.c. k____   3.d. d____

4.a. l____   4.b. q____   4.c. t____   4.d. x____

5.a. f____   5.b. p____   5.c. x____   5.d. j____

6.a. b____   6.b. j____   6.c. q____   6.d. t____

7.a. l____   7.b. g____   7.c. q____   7.d. x____

IV. Neutral Tones

Listen to the CD and mark the tone marks.

A.1. guanxi   A.2. kuzi   A.3. shifu   A.4. keqi

B.1. zhuozi   B.2. gaosu   B.3. shufu   B.4. women

C.1. gege   C.2. weizi   C.3. dongxi   C.4. yisi

D.1. nimen   D.2. shihou   D.3. chuqu   D.4. pengyou

E.1. meimei   E.2. xihuan   E.3. jiaozi   E.4. xiansheng

F.1. zenme   F.2. didi   F.3. erzi   F.4. xiexie

G.1. jiejie   G.2. mafan   G.3. bobo   G.4. yizi

V. Exercises for Initials, Finals, and Tones: Monosyllabic Words

Transcribe what you hear into pinyin with tone marks.

A.1._____   A.2. _____   A.3._____   A.4._____

B.1._____   B.2._____   B.3._____   B.4._____

C.1._____   C.2._____   C.3._____   C.4._____

D.1._____   D.2._____   D.3._____   D.4._____

E.1._____   E.2._____   E.3._____   E.4._____

F.1._____   F.2._____   F.3._____   F.4._____

G.1._____   G.2._____   G.3._____   G.4._____

H.1._____   H.2._____   H.3._____   H.4._____

I.1._____   I.2._____   I.3._____   I.4._____

VI. Exercises for Initials, Finals, and Tones: Bisyllabic Words

Put the letter corresponding to the word you hear into the parentheses.

( ) A.1. a. làoshī   b. lǎoshī   c. lǎoshí

( ) A.2. a. Méiguó   b. Měiguó   c. Mèiguó

( ) A.3. a. zhàopiàn   b. zhāopiàn   c. zháopiàn

( ) A.4. a. wànfàn   b. wǎnfān   c. wǎnfàn

( ) B.1. a. shēngrì   b. shéngrì   c. shěngrì

( ) B.2. a. zāijiàn   b. zàijiàn   c. záijiàn

( ) B.3. a. xuéshēng   b. xuèsheng   c. xuésheng

( ) B.4. a. diànyǐng   b. diānyǐng   c. diànyìng

( ) C.1. a. zuòtiān   b. zuótiān   c. zuótiàn

( ) C.2. a. suírán   b. suīrán   c. suīràn

( ) C.3. a. xièxiè   b. shèshe   c. xièxie

( ) C.4. a. kāfēi   b. káfēi   c. kāifēi

( ) D.1. a. kělè   b. kělè   c. kělà

( ) D.2. a. píngcháng   b. pēngchán   c. píngchèng

( ) D.3. a. gōngzuò   b. gōngzhuò   c. gōngzòu

( ) D.4. a. piàoliàng   b. piāoliang   c. piàoliang

( ) E.1. a. fángbiàn   b. fāngbián   c. fāngbiàn

( ) E.2. a. wèntì   b. wèntí   c. wěntí

( ) E.3. a. fùxí   b. fùxi   c. fǔxí

( ) E.4. a. rōngyì   b. lóngyì   c. róngyì

▼▼

( ) F.1. a. kāishǐ   b. kāixǐ   c. kāisǐ

( ) F.2. a. loùdiǎn   b. liùdiǎn   c. liùdǎn

( ) F.3. a. píjiǔ   b. pìjiǔ   c. peíjiǔ

( ) F.4. a. nǔ'ér   b. nǔ'èr   c. nǚ'ér

VII. Exercises for Initials, Finals, and Tones: Cities

Read the following words and identify which cities they are. Put the letter corresponding to the city name into the parentheses.

Example: Mài'āmì   →   <u>Miami</u>

( )   1. Bōshìdùn   a. Venice

( )   2. Lúndūn   b. Toronto

( )   3. Niǔyuē   c. Boston

( )   4. Bālí   d. Chicago

( )   5. Zhījiāgē   e. Seattle

( )   6. Běijīng   f. New York

( )   7. Luòshānjī   g. Paris

( )   8. Duōlúnduō   h. London

( )   9. Xīyǎtú   i. Beijing

( )   10. Wēinísī   j. Los Angeles

VIII. Exercises for Initials, Finals, and Tones: Celebrities

Read the following words and write each celebrity's name in English.

1. Mǎdānnà   _____

2. Màikè Jiékèsēn   _____

3. Yīlìshābái Tàilè   _____

4. Bābālā Sīcuìshān   _____

5. Aòdàilì Hèběn   _____

6. Suǒfēiyǎ Luólán   _____

7. Mǎlìlián Mènglù   _____

▼ ▼

IX. Exercises for Initials, Finals, and Tones: Countries

Transcribe what you hear into pinyin with tone marks and write each country name in English.

Example: <u>Rìběn</u> → <u>Japan</u>

1._____ → _____
2._____ → _____
3._____ → _____
4._____ → _____
5._____ → _____
6._____ → _____
7._____ → _____
8._____ → _____
9._____ → _____
10._____ → _____

X. Exercises for Initials, Finals, and Tones: American Presidents

Transcribe what you hear into pinyin with tone marks and write down each president's name in English.

1._____ → _____
2._____ → _____
3._____ → _____
4._____ → _____
5._____ → _____
6._____ → _____
7._____ → _____
8._____ → _____
9._____ → _____
10._____ → _____

LESSON 1 ▲ Greetings
第一课 ▲ 问好
Dì yí kè ▲ *Wèn hǎo*

Part One

DIALOGUE I: EXCHANGING GREETINGS

I. Listening Comprehension

A. Textbook Dialogue I (Multiple Choice)

(   ) 1. What was the first thing that the man said to the woman?

    a. What's your name?   b. I'm Mr. Wang.

    c. Are you Miss Li?   d. How do you do!

(   ) 2. What is the woman's full name?

    a. Wang Peng   b. Li You

    c. Xing Li   d. Jiao Li You

(   ) 3. What is the man's full name?

    a. Wang Peng   b. Li You

    c. Xing Wang   d. Jiao Wang Peng

B. Workbook Dialogue I (Multiple Choice)

(   ) These two people are:

    a. saying good-bye to each other.

    b. asking each other's name.

    c. greeting each other.

    d. asking each other's nationality.

C. Workbook Dialogue II (Multiple Choice)

(   ) 1. The two speakers are most likely:

    a. brother and sister.

    b. father and daughter.

    c. old friends reuniting.

    d. strangers getting acquainted.

( ) 2. Who are these two people?

    a. Mr. Li and Miss You

    b. Mr. Li and Miss Li

    c. Mr. Wang and Miss You

    d. Mr. Wang and Miss Wang

II. SPEAKING EXERCISES

A. Answer the questions in Chinese based on Textbook Dialogue I.

1. How does Mr. Wang greet Miss Li in Chinese?

2. What is Miss Li's reply?

3. How does Mr. Wang ask what Miss Li's surname is?

4. What is Mr. Wang's given name?

5. How does Mr. Wang ask what Miss Li's given name is?

6. What is Miss Li's given name?

B. You meet a Chinese student on campus:

1. Greet him/her in Chinese.

2. Ask his/her name.

▼ ▼

III. READING COMPREHENSION

Read the passage and answer the questions. (True/False)

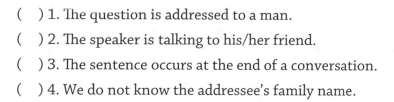

你好，先生。请问您贵姓？

Questions:

    (   ) 1. The question is addressed to a man.

    (   ) 2. The speaker is talking to his/her friend.

    (   ) 3. The sentence occurs at the end of a conversation.

    (   ) 4. We do not know the addressee's family name.

IV. WRITING & GRAMMAR EXERCISES

Grammar and Usage

A. Give the Chinese characters for the following sentences in pinyin.

    1. Nín guì xìng?

    2. Nǐ jiào shénme míngzi?

B. Rearrange the given Chinese words into a sentence, using the English sentence as a clue.

叫 / 名字 / 你 / 请问 / 什么

(May I ask what your name is?)

C. Answer the following questions in Chinese.

1. 您贵姓？

2.你叫什么名字?

Translation

Translate the following sentences, making use of the Chinese words or phrases in parentheses.

1. May I ask what your surname is? (请问,贵姓)

2. My surname is Li. My name is Li You. (我姓...,我叫...)

Writing Practice

Write your Chinese name, if you have one, in characters.

▼ ▼

Part Two

DIALOGUE II: ASKING ONE'S STATUS

I. Listening Comprehension

A. Textbook Dialogue II (True/False)

Quote the key sentence from the dialogue to support your answer.

(   ) 1. Miss Li is a student.

(   ) 2. Mr. Wang is a teacher.

(   ) 3. Mr. Wang is an American.

(   ) 4. Miss Li is a Chinese.

B. Workbook Dialogue III (Multiple Choice)

(   ) Which of the following is true?

     a. Both the man and the woman are Chinese.

     b. Both the man and the woman are American.

     c. The man is Chinese and the woman is American.

     d. The man is American and the woman is Chinese.

C. Workbook Dialogue IV (Multiple Choice)

(   ) Which of the following is true?

     a. Both the man and the woman are teachers.

     b. Both the man and the woman are students.

     c. The man is a teacher. The woman is a student.

     d. The man is a student. The woman is a teacher.

II. Speaking Exercises

A. Answer the questions in Chinese based on Textbook Dialogue II.

1. How does Miss Li ask whether Mr. Wang is a teacher or not?

2. Is Mr. Wang a teacher?

3. Is Miss Li a teacher?

4. What is Mr. Wang's nationality?

5. What is Miss Li's nationality?

B. You meet a middle-aged Chinese person on campus. Try to ask politely in Chinese whether he/she is a teacher.

C. Introduce yourself in Chinese to a Chinese student. Tell him/her what your name is and whether you are a student.

D. You just met a foreign student who can speak Chinese.

    1. Ask him/her whether he/she is Chinese.

    2. Tell him/her that you are American.

III. Reading Comprehension

A. Read the passage and answer the questions. (True/False)

王小姐是中国学生。李先生是美国老师。

Questions:

( ) 1. 王小姐姓王。

( ) 2. 王小姐是美国人。

( ) 3. 王小姐不是老师。

( ) 4. 李先生不是中国人。

( ) 5. 李先生是老师。

B. Match the utterances on the left column with the appropriate responses on the right column. Write down the letter in the parentheses.

( ) 1. 你好！   A. 是，我是老师。

( ) 2. 您贵姓？   B. 不，我是中国人。

( ) 3. 你是美国人吗？ C. 我也是学生。

( ) 4. 你是老师吗？   D. 我姓李。

( ) 5. 我是学生，你呢？ E. 你好

▼ ▼

C. Based on your understanding of the passage below, fill out of the following form in English. Then answer the questions below.

王先生叫王中师。王中师是美国人，不是中国人。王中师是学生，不是老师。李小姐叫李美生。李美生是中国老师，不是美国学生。

	Gender	Given name	Nationality	Occupation
王先生				
李小姐				

Questions (Multiple Choice):

(　) 1. If you were the man's close friend, most often you would address him as:

    a. Wang Xiansheng.

    b. Xiansheng Wang.

    c. Wang.

    d. Zhongshi.

(　) 2. If you were being introduced to the woman for the first time, it would be most appropriate for you to address her as:

    a. Li Xiaojie.

    b. Xiaojie Li.

    c. Li Meisheng.

    d. Meisheng.

D. Chinese Business Cards

Below are four Chinese business cards. Circle all of the characters that you recognize, and underline the characters denoting family names.

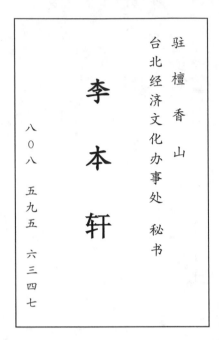

驻 檀 香 山
台 北 经 济 文 化 办 事 处　秘 书

李 本 轩

八 〇 八　五 九 五　六 三 四 七

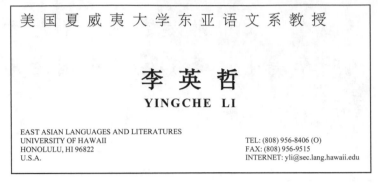

美 国 夏 威 夷 大 学 东 亚 语 文 系 教 授

李 英 哲
YINGCHE LI

EAST ASIAN LANGUAGES AND LITERATURES
UNIVERSITY OF HAWAII
HONOLULU, HI 96822
U.S.A.

TEL: (808) 956-8406 (O)
FAX: (808) 956-9515
INTERNET: yli@sec.lang.hawaii.edu

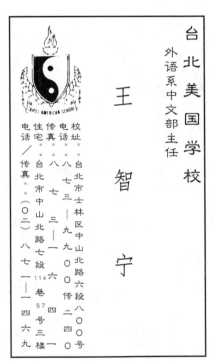

台 北 美 国 学 校
外 语 系 中 文 部 主 任

王 智 宁

中 外 合 资
常 州 华 润 装 饰 工 程 有 限 公 司
CHANGZHOU HUA RUN DECORATION ENGINEERING CO. LTD.

王 德 中
WANG DE ZHONG
董事　副总经理

地址：中国常州劳动中路４２号
ADD: N°42 LAO DONG RD(M) CHANGZHOU
电话　TEL: 8824743　8813361
传真　FAX: 0519--8824743
电挂　CABLE: 5000　邮编　P C:213001
宅电　HOME: 6622599

IV. Writing & Grammar Exercises

Grammar and Usage

A. Give the Chinese characters for the following sentences in pinyin.

1. Qǐng wèn, nǐ shì xuésheng ma?

2. Wǒ shì Zhōngguórén. Nǐ ne?

▼▼▼▼▼▼▼▼▼▼▼▼▼▼▼▼▼▼▼▼▼▼▼▼▼▼▼▼▼▼▼▼▼▼▼▼▼▼

3. Wǒ bú xìng Wáng, wǒ xìng Lǐ.

4. Nín shì lǎoshī, wǒ shì xuésheng.

5. Nǐ shì Měiguórén, wǒ yě shì Měiguórén.

B. Rearrange the given Chinese words into a sentence, using the English sentence as a clue.

1. 姓 / 王 / 吗 / 你
(Is your surname Wang?)

2. 吗 / 是 / 你 / 学生 / 美国
(Are you an American student?)

3. 中国 / 是 / 人 / 我 / 不
(I am not Chinese.)

4. 小姐 / 先生 / 美国人 / 美国人 / 王 /
李 / 也 / 是 / 是
(Miss Li is American. Mr. Wang is also American.)

C. Answer the following questions in Chinese.

1. 你是学生吗？

2. 李小姐是美国人。你呢？

3. 王先生是中国学生。你呢？

D. Form the questions that would elicit the following statements.

Example: 我是学生。 →你是学生吗？

1. 我是美国人。

2. 我姓李。

3. 王老师是中国人。

4. 李小姐不是学生。

5. 我也是学生。

E. In each group, use 也 *to connect the two sentences into a compound sentence.*

Example: 李友是学生。/王朋是学生。
→李友是学生，王朋也是学生。

1. 你是美国人。／我是美国人。

2. 李小姐不是中国人。／李先生不是中国人。

3. 你不姓王。／我不姓王。

4. 王先生是老师。／李小姐是老师。

Translation

Translate the following sentences into Chinese, using the words or phrases in parentheses.

1. I am American. （是）

2. Are you Chinese? （是，吗）

3. I am a teacher. How about you? （呢）

4.*A:* I am an American student. Are you an American student, too? （也）

   B: No, I am a Chinese student. （不）

5. Mr. Wang is not Chinese. Nor am I. (也不)

[Note: The following sentences contain supplementary vocabulary.]

6. May I ask if you are Japanese?

7. Mr. Wang is English. Mrs. Wang is Chinese.

8. Mr. Li is not French. Mrs. Li is not French, either.

Writing Practice

Without looking at the book, write as many characters as you can from Lesson 1.

LESSON 2 ▲ Family
第二课 ▲ 家庭
Dì èr kè ▲ *Jiātíng*

DIALOGUE I: LOOKING AT A FAMILY PHOTO

I. Listening Comprehension

A. Textbook Dialogue I (True/False)

Quote the key sentence from the dialogue to support your answer.

( ) 1. The picture in question belongs to Wang Peng.

( ) 2. Little Gao doesn't have any younger brothers.

( ) 3. Little Gao's parents are in the picture.

( ) 4. All the people in the picture are members of Little Gao's family.

( ) 5. Mr. Li does not have any sons.

B. Workbook Dialogue I (Multiple Choice)

( ) Who are the people in the picture?

   a. The woman's father and mother.

   b. The woman's mother and younger sister.

   c. The woman's older sister and younger sister.

   d. The woman's mother and older sister.

II. Speaking Exercises

A. Answer the questions in Chinese based on Textbook Dialogue I.

1. Whose photo is on the wall?

2. How many people are there in Little Gao's family? Who are they?

3. Is the boy in the picture Little Gao's younger brother? How do you know?

4. Is the girl in the picture Little Gao's younger sister? How do you know?

▼▼▼▼▼▼▼▼▼▼▼▼▼▼▼▼▼▼▼▼▼▼▼▼▼▼▼▼▼▼▼

B. Find a picture of your parents and use it to introduce your parents to your friends.

III. Reading Comprehension

A. Match the questions on the left with the appropriate replies on the right. Write down the letter in the parentheses.

( ) 1. 这个人是谁？　　A. 是我的。

( ) 2. 这张照片是谁的？　　B. 这是我爸爸。

( ) 3. 你妹妹是学生吗？　　C. 他有儿子，没有 女儿。

( ) 4. 李先生有女儿吗？　　D. 我没有弟弟。

( ) 5. 你有弟弟吗？　　E. 她是学生。

B. Read the following dialogue and answer the questions.

(Li You is nearsighted.)

王朋：李友，这张照片是你的吗？

李友：是。这是我爸爸，这是我妈妈。

王朋：这个女孩子是谁？

李友：是我 . . . (looking at the picture again more carefully)

　　　不是，不是，　这不是我。

王朋：她是你妹妹吗？

李友：也不是。她是高小姐。这是高小姐 的照片，不是我的。

Questions (Multiple Choice):

( ) 1. Which of the following is correct?

　　　a. Li You was looking at someone else's photo but mistook it for her own.

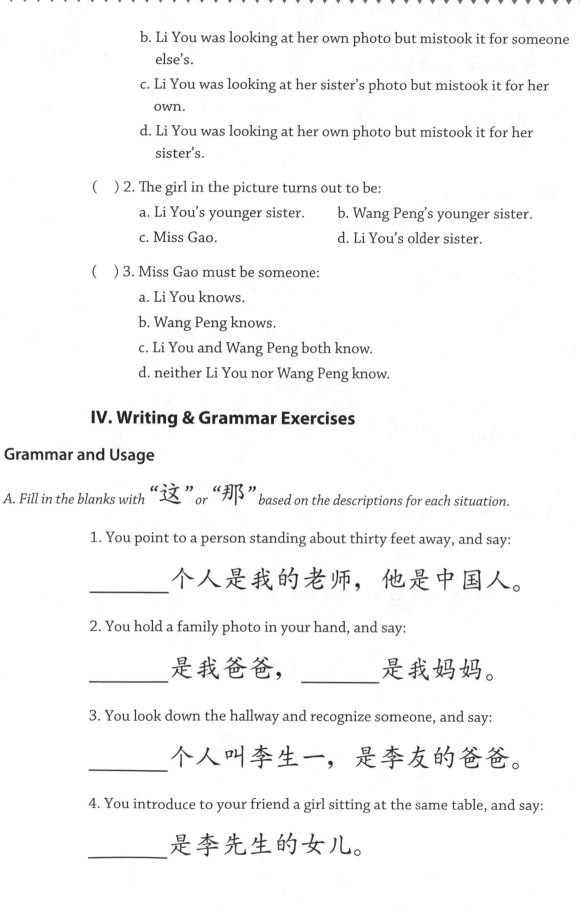

      b. Li You was looking at her own photo but mistook it for someone else's.

      c. Li You was looking at her sister's photo but mistook it for her own.

      d. Li You was looking at her own photo but mistook it for her sister's.

(   ) 2. The girl in the picture turns out to be:

      a. Li You's younger sister.   b. Wang Peng's younger sister.

      c. Miss Gao.   d. Li You's older sister.

(   ) 3. Miss Gao must be someone:

      a. Li You knows.

      b. Wang Peng knows.

      c. Li You and Wang Peng both know.

      d. neither Li You nor Wang Peng know.

IV. Writing & Grammar Exercises

Grammar and Usage

A. Fill in the blanks with "这" *or* "那" *based on the descriptions for each situation.*

1. You point to a person standing about thirty feet away, and say:

    _____个人是我的老师，他是中国人。

2. You hold a family photo in your hand, and say:

    _____是我爸爸，_____是我妈妈。

3. You look down the hallway and recognize someone, and say:

    _____个人叫李生一，是李友的爸爸。

4. You introduce to your friend a girl sitting at the same table, and say:

    _____是李先生的女儿。

Translation

Translate the following sentences into Chinese, using the words or phrases in parentheses.

1. Little Wang, is this photograph yours? （是…吗？）

2. Mr. Wang has no sons.

3. Is this person your mother?

4. Is this boy your younger brother?

5. *A:* Who is this person? （谁）

   B: She's my younger sister. （是）

6. *A:* Do you have any younger brothers? （有）

   B: No, I don't have any younger brothers. （没有）

Writing Practice

Without looking at the textbook, write as many characters as you can from Lesson 2, Dialogue I.

▼▼

Part Two

DIALOGUE II: ASKING ABOUT SOMEONE'S FAMILY

I. Listening Comprehension

A. Textbook Dialogue II (Multiple Choice)

( ) 1. How many people are there in Little Zhang's family?

    a. 3   b. 4   c. 5   d. 6

( ) 2. How many people are there in Li You's family?

    a. 3   b. 4   c. 5   d. 6

( ) 3. How many older sisters does Little Zhang have?

    a. 0   b. 1   c. 2   d. 3

( ) 4. How many younger sisters does Li You have?

    a. 0   b. 1   c. 2   d. 3

( ) 5. How many older brothers does Little Zhang have?

    a. 0   b. 1   c. 2   d. 3

( ) 6. How many younger brothers does Little Zhang have?

    a. 0   b. 1   c. 2   d. 3

( ) 7. How many children do Little Zhang's parents have?

    a. 2   b. 3   c. 4   d. 5

( ) 8. How many sons do Li You's parents have?

    a. 0   b. 1   c. 2   d. 3

( ) 9. Little Zhang's father is a:

    a. lawyer.   b. teacher.   c. doctor.   d. student.

( ) 10. Li You's mother is a:

    a. lawyer.   b. teacher.   c. doctor.   d. student.

B. Workbook Dialogue II (Multiple Choice)

( ) 1. Which of the following is true?

    a. Both the man and the woman have older brothers.

    b. Both the man and the woman have younger brothers.

c. The man has an older brother but no younger brothers.

d. The man has a younger brother but no older brothers.

( ) 2. Why does the woman laugh at the end of the conversation? Because she finds it funny that:

a. neither the man nor she herself has any younger brothers.

b. neither the man nor she herself has any older brothers.

c. the man failed to count himself as his older brother's younger brother.

d. the man failed to count himself as his younger brother's older brother.

C. Workbook Dialogue III (Multiple Choice)

( ) 1. The man's mother is a:

a. teacher.   b. student.   c. doctor.   d. lawyer.

( ) 2. The woman's father is a:

a. teacher.   b. student.   c. doctor.   d. lawyer.

D. Workbook Dialogue IV (Multiple Choice)

( ) 1. How many brothers does the woman have?

a. 1   b. 2   c. 3   d. 4

( ) 2. How many daughters do the woman's parents have?

a. 1   b. 2   c. 3   d. 4

( ) 3. How many people in the woman's family are older than herself?

a. 2   b. 3   c. 4   d. 5

( ) 4. How many people in the man's family are younger than himself?

a. 0   b. 1   c. 2   d. 3

( ) 5. Why do the speakers disagree on the number of people in the man's family? Because he forgot to include:

a. his older brother.   b. his younger sister.

c. his younger brother.   d. himself.

II. Speaking Exercises

A. Answer the questions in Chinese based on Textbook Dialogue II.

1. How many people are there in Little Zhang's family?

2. How many children do Little Zhang's parents have?

3. What is the birth order of Little Zhang?

4. How many brothers and sisters does Li You have?

5. What is the occupation of Little Zhang's father?

6. What is the occupation of Little Zhang's mother and Li You's mother?

7. How many people are there in Li You's family?

8. How many daughters do Li You's parents have?

B. Find a family picture and use it to introduce your family members to your friends.

C. Show your family photo to your partner and ask questions about each other's photo, such as who the person is, whether your partner has any brothers or sisters, what each of his/her family members does.

D. Following are four members of Wang You's family. Introduce them. Make sure that you mention what they do.

1. Wang You's older brother

2. Wang You's mother

3. Wang You's father

4. Wang You's younger brother

III. Reading Comprehension

A. This is a family portrait of the Gao family. Look at the photo carefully and identify each person.

1. 爸爸 （　）   2. 妈妈 （　）

3. 妹妹 （　）   4. 弟弟 （　）

B. Match each Chinese word with its English equivalent by placing the letter in the appropriate parentheses.

（　）1. 爸爸   A. mother

（　）2. 哥哥   B. younger sister

（　）3. 弟弟   C. older sister

（　）4. 妹妹   D. older brother

（　）5. 妈妈   E. younger brother

（　）6. 姐姐   F. father

（　）7. 谁   G. how many

（　）8. 几   H. who

（　）9. 谁的   I. whose

C. Read the passage and answer the questions. (True/False)

小高家有五个人，爸爸、妈妈、一个姐姐、一个妹妹和他。他的爸爸是医生，妈妈是律师，姐姐是老师，他和妹妹都是学生。

Questions:

（　）1. Little Gao has two sisters.

（　）2. Little Gao has one brother.

（　）3. Little Gao is the youngest child in his family.

（　）4. Little Gao's parents have three children.

（　）5. Little Gao's parents are both doctors.

（　）6. Little Gao's sisters are both teachers.

（　）7. Little Gao is a student.

D. Read the passage and answer the questions. (True/False)

小王家有六个人。她的爸爸是老师，妈妈
是医生。她有一个哥哥、两个妹妹。她的
哥哥也是医生，她和两个妹妹都是学生。

Questions:

(   ) 1. Little Wang is the oldest child in the family.

(   ) 2. Little Wang's father and her brother are both teachers.

(   ) 3. Little Wang's parents have only one son.

(   ) 4. Little Wang's mother and brother are both doctors.

(   ) 5. All the girls in the Wang family are students.

E. Based on your understanding of the passage below, fill out of the following form in English. Then answer the questions below. (True/False)

小王：请问，你爸爸是律师吗？

小高：不，他是老师。我家有两个老师，
　　　三个医生。

小王：你家有五个人吗？

小高：不，我家有四个人。我和我妈妈都
　　　是医生。我哥哥是老师，也是医生。

Mark the proper spaces in the following form to indicate the profession of each member of Xiao Gao's family:

	Xiao Gao	Father	Mother	Brother
Lawyer				
Doctor				
Teacher				

Questions:

(   ) 1. Xiao Wang seems to know Xiao Gao's family very well.

(   ) 2. Xiao Gao seems to have miscounted the people in his family.

(   ) 3. Xiao Gao's older brother is not only a teacher, but also a doctor.

IV. Writing & Grammar Exercises

Grammar and Usage

A. Answer the following questions about your siblings in complete sentences, using 有 *or* 没有 *. If the answer is positive, state how many there are.*

Examples: 1.A: 你有哥哥吗？   B: 我没有哥哥。

2.A: 你有哥哥吗？   B: 我有三个哥哥。

1.A: 你有姐姐吗？

B: _____。

2.A: 你有妹妹吗？

B: _____。

3.A: 你有弟弟吗？

B: _____。

4.A: 你有哥哥吗？

B: _____。

B. Rewrite the following sentences using 都 *.*

Example: 小高是学生，王朋也是学生。

→ 小高、王朋都是学生。

1. 小高有姐姐，小张也有姐姐。

2. 王朋是学生，李友也是学生。

3. 这张照片是你的，那张照片也是你的。

4. 这个人姓李，那个人也姓李。

5. 李友没有我的照片，王朋也没有我的照片。

6. 他哥哥不是律师，他弟弟也不是律师。

7. 王朋有哥哥，小高有哥哥，李友有哥哥。

8. 我爸爸是医生，我妈妈是医生，我哥哥是律师。

C. *Fill in the blanks with the appropriate question words.* （什么、谁、谁的、几）

1.A:_____名字叫王朋？   B: 他的名字叫王朋。

2.A:李老师家有_____个人？   B: 他家有三个人。

3.A:你爸爸是做_____的？   B: 我爸爸是医生。

4.A:你妹妹叫_____名字？   B: 我妹妹叫高美美。

5.A:那个美国人是_____？   B: 他叫 David Smith, 是我的老师。

6.A: 你有 _____张你妈妈的   B: 我有两张。
照片？

Translation

Translate the following sentences into Chinese, using the words or phrases in parentheses.

1. Mr. Zhang has three daughters.

2.A: Is he your older brother?

B: No, he's my father. （不是）

3.A: How many older sisters do you have? （有，几）

B: I have two older sisters.

4.A: How many people are there in your family? （有，几）

B: There are six people in my family: my dad, my mom, two older brothers,
a younger sister and I. （有）

5.A: What do your older brothers and older sisters do? （什么）

▼▼

B: My older brothers and older sisters are all students.

6.*A:* My mom is a lawyer. My dad is a doctor. How about your mom and dad? （呢）

B: My mom is a lawyer, too. My dad is a teacher. （也）

7. Both my teacher and her teacher are Americans.

8. Neither Little Gao nor Little Zhang is Chinese.

Writing Practice

A. List your family members in Chinese.

B. To the best of your Chinese ability, tell what each of your family members does.

C. Write a paragraph describing the picture above.

One possible answer:

This is Little Zhang's picture. Little Zhang is my friend. He is Chinese. He is a teacher. He has three students.

LESSON 3 ▲ Dates and Time
第三课 ▲ 时间
Dì sān kè ▲ *Shíjiān*

Part One

DIALOGUE I: TAKING SOMEONE OUT TO EAT ON HIS/HER BIRTHDAY

I. Listening Comprehension

A. Textbook Dialogue I (True/False)

Quote the key sentence from the dialogue to support your answer.

( ) 1. Little Gao will be eighteen years old this year.

( ) 2. September 12 is Thursday.

( ) 3. Little Bai will treat Little Gao to a dinner on Thursday.

( ) 4. Little Gao is American. Therefore, he likes American food.

( ) 5. Little Bai refuses to eat American food.

( ) 6. They will have dinner together at 6:30 p.m.

B. Workbook Dialogue I (Multiple Choice)

( ) 1. Today's date is:

    a. May 10.   b. June 10.   c. October 5.   d. October 6.

( ) 2. What day is today?

    a. Thursday   b. Friday   c. Saturday   d. Sunday

( ) 3. What day is October 7?

    a. Thursday   b. Friday   c. Saturday   d. Sunday

C. Workbook Dialogue II (Multiple Choice)

( ) 1. What time does the man propose to meet?

    a. 6:30   b. 7:00   c. 7:30   d. 8:00

( ) 2. What time do they finally agree upon?

    a. 6:30   b. 7:00   c. 7:30   d. 8:00

( ) 3. What day are they going to meet?

      a. Thursday   b. Friday   c. Saturday   d. Sunday

II. Speaking Exercises

A. Answer the following questions in Chinese based on Textbook Dialogue I.

1. When is Little Gao's birthday?
2. How old is Little Gao?
3. Who is going to treat whom?
4. What is Little Gao's nationality?
5. What kind of dinner are they going to have?
6. What time is the dinner?

B. Tomorrow is your partner's birthday. Find out how old he/she is and offer to take him/her out to dinner. Ask him/her if he/she prefers Chinese or American food and decide upon the time for the dinner.

III. Reading Comprehension

A. Read the sentences and answer the questions. (Multiple Choice)

( ) 1. 今天星期六，明天星期几？

      a. Thursday   b. Friday   c. Saturday   d. Sunday

( ) 2. 十月二号星期四，十月四号星期几？

      a. 星期四   b. 星期五   c. 星期六   d. 星期日

B. Fill in the blanks below in English based on the calendar.

2005 年

九 月

22 日

星期一

The date on this calendar is _____.

The day of the week is _____.

Next month is _____.

The day after tomorrow is a _____.

C. Which of the following is the correct way to say "June 3, 1997" in Chinese? Circle the correct answer.

1. 六月三日一九九七年
2. 三日六月一九九七年
3. 六月一九九七年三日
4. 一九九七年六月三日

D. Read the following dialogue and answer the questions. (True/False)

小高：小王，你喜欢吃中国饭还是美国饭？

小王：我喜欢吃中国饭。

小高：我请你吃中国饭怎么样？

小王：太好了，谢谢。你星期几请我吃饭？

小高：星期六晚上，怎么样？

小王：星期六晚上我很忙。

小高：为什么？

小王：因为那天晚上我请李友吃晚饭。

Questions:

(　) 1. Xiao Wang likes Chinese food better than American food.

(　) 2. Xiao Gao offers to take Xiao Wang to dinner.

(　) 3. Most likely Xiao Wang and Xiao Gao will not have dinner together on Saturday.

(　) 4. Li You will treat Xiao Wang to dinner Saturday evening.

IV. Writing & Grammar Exercises

Grammar and Usage

A. Write the following numbers using Chinese characters.

1. 15 _____   2. 93 _____

3. 47 _____   4. 62 _____

5. Your phone number _____

B. Compose questions to elicit the following answers. Use 还是 *in each question.*

Example: A: 王朋是中国人还是美国人？

B: 王朋是中国人。

1.A: _____?

B: 我喜欢吃美国饭。

2.A: _____?

B: 小白是小高的同学。

3.A: _____?

B: 小张的爸爸是律师。

5.A: _____?

B: 李友是老师。

6.A: _____?

B: 星期二是我的生日。

▼▼▼

C. Rearrange the following Chinese words into sentences, using the English sentences as clues.

1. 我 / 吃饭 / 今天 / 你 / 怎么样 / 晚上 / 请

How would it be if I take you out to dinner this evening?

2. 星期四 / 星期五 / 吃饭 / 我 / 你 / 还是 / 请

Is it Thursday or Friday that you are going to take me out to dinner?

3. 哥哥 / 小张 / 喜欢 / 他的 / 我 / 我 / 可是 / 不 / 喜欢

I do not like Little Zhang, but I like his older brother.

4. 美国人 / 美国饭 / 可是 / 他 / 不 / 喜欢 / 吃 / 是 / 他

He is American, but he does not like to eat American food.

Translation

Translate the following sentences into Chinese, using the words or phrases in parentheses.

1. What day of the week is June 3? (几)

2. Whose birthday is August 7? (谁的)

3. What month and day is your dad's birthday? （几）

4. How old is Little Gao (this year)? （多大）

5. Is Wang Peng Chinese or American? （还是）

6. Little Bai is American, but he likes to eat Chinese food. （可是）

7. In my family, there are Dad, Mom, a younger brother and I.

Writing Practice

A. Write today's date in Chinese.

B. Write the current time in Chinese.

▼▼

Part Two

DIALOGUE II: INVITING SOMEONE TO DINNER

I. Listening Comprehension

A. Textbook Dialogue II (True/False)

Quote the key sentence from the dialogue to support your answer.

( ) 1. Wang Peng will not be free until 6:15.

( ) 2. Wang Peng will not be busy tomorrow.

( ) 3. Little Bai is inviting Wang Peng to dinner.

( ) 4. Tomorrow is Little Bai's birthday.

( ) 5. Wang Peng doesn't know Little Gao.

( ) 6. Little Li is Little Bai's schoolmate.

( ) 7. Wang Peng doesn't know Little Li.

B. Workbook Dialogue III (True/False)

Quote the key sentence from the dialogue to support your answer.

( ) 1. Both speakers in the dialogue are Chinese.

( ) 2. The man invites the woman to dinner because it will be his birthday tomorrow.

( ) 3. The man likes Chinese food.

( ) 4. The woman does not like Chinese food.

C. Workbook Dialogue IV (True/False)

Quote the key sentence from the dialogue to support your answer.

( ) 1. Today the woman is busy.

( ) 2. Today the man is not busy.

( ) 3. Tomorrow both the man and the woman will be very busy.

II. Speaking Exercises

A. Answer the questions in Chinese based on Textbook Dialogue II.

1. Why does Little Bai ask if Wang Peng is busy or not?

2. When is Wang Peng busy?

3. Who else will go out for dinner tomorrow with Little Bai and Wang Peng?

4. Does Little Bai know Little Li? How do you know?

B. Invite a mutual friend to join you and your partner for dinner. Explain what the occasion is and who else will be there.

C. Your partner would like to take you out to dinner on your birthday, but you will be very busy that day. Suggest another day for the dinner and decide on a time.

III. Reading Comprehension

A. Write the following times in ordinary numeral notation (e.g., 1:00, 2:40, 3:10 p.m.).

1. 三点钟：_____

2. 两点十分：_____

3. 六点五十分：_____

4. 晚上八点钟：_____

5. 晚上九点一刻：_____

6. 晚上十一点半：_____

B. Read the passage and answer the questions. (True/False)

明天是小白的同学小高的生日。小白和他姐姐请小高吃饭，因为小白的姐姐也认识小高。小高是美国人，可是他喜欢吃中国饭。明天晚上他们吃中国饭。

Questions:

( ) 1. Tomorrow is Little Bai's birthday.

( ) 2. Little Bai's sister knows Little Gao.

( ) 3. Little Gao and Little Bai are classmates.

( ) 4. Little Gao is Chinese.

( ) 5. Little Gao likes Chinese food.

( ) 6. Little Gao is going to pay for the dinner.

C. Read the passage and answer the questions. (True/False)

李小姐、白小姐和高先生是同学。今天是李小姐的生日，晚上六点半白小姐和高先生的妹妹请她吃晚饭，可是李小姐不认识高先生的妹妹。

Questions:

( ) 1. Miss Li and Miss Bai are classmates.

( ) 2. Miss Li is going to treat Miss Bai to dinner tonight.

( ) 3. Today is Miss Li's birthday.

( ) 4. Miss Li will not have dinner at home this evening.

( ) 5. Miss Li will see Mr. Gao at 6:30 p.m.

( ) 6. Miss Li and Mr. Gao's younger sister are close friends.

D. Read the following dialogue and answer the questions. (Multiple Choice)

小白：今天是几月几号？

小李：今天是二月二十八号。

小白：是吗？明天是我的生日。我的生日是二月二十九号。明天晚上我请你吃晚饭，怎么样？

小李： 太好了,谢谢。可是明天不是二月二
　　　 十九号。

小白： 那明天是几月几号?

小李： 明天是三月一号。你今年没有生日。

Questions:

( ) 1. Which of the following statements is true?

a. Xiao Bai has been expecting her birthday all week.

b. Xiao Bai almost failed to realize that her birthday was approaching.

c. Xiao Li has been expecting Xiao Bai's birthday.

( ) 2. Tomorrow will be:

a. February 28.   b. February 29.   c. March 1.

( ) 3. Which of the following statements is true?

a. Xiao Bai has forgotten her birthday.

b. Xiao Li gave the wrong date for tomorrow.

c. Xiao Bai's birthday is off this year's calendar.

IV. Writing & Grammar Exercises

Grammar and Usage

A. Turn the following dates or time phrases into Chinese using Chinese characters.

1. November 12 _____

2. Friday evening _____

3. 7:00 this evening _____

4. 8:30 p.m. Saturday _____

5. quarter after nine _____

B. Complete the following exchanges.

1.A: 今天是几月几号？

　B: _____。

2.A: 你的生日是 _____？

　B: 我的生日是 _____。

3.A: 你今年多大？

　B: _____。

4.A: 现在几点钟？

　B: 现在 _____ 点 _____ 分。

5.A: _____？

　B: 我五点三刻吃晚饭。

C. Compose questions using the "A-not-A" form that would elicit the following answers.

Example:　A: 王朋明天有没有事？

　　　　B: 王朋明天没有事。

1.A: _____？

　B: 王先生是中国人。

2.A: _____？

　B: 小高没有弟弟。

3.A: _____？

　B: 小高喜欢吃美国饭。

4.A: _____？

　B: 王朋明天不忙。

5. A: _____?

    B: 小张的爸爸不是医生。

D. Based on the text, answer the following questions with 因为 .

    1. 小白为什么请小高吃饭?

    2. 小白为什么不请小高吃中国饭?

    3. 小白为什么问王朋忙不忙?

    4. 小白为什么认识小李?

Translation

Translate the following sentences into Chinese, using the words or phrases in parentheses.

    1. Who will you invite to dinner on Monday evening? (谁)

    2. A: When are we having dinner tomorrow evening? (几点钟)

      B: Half past seven.

    3. Little Zhang, will you be busy Thursday evening? (V + 不 + V)

4. We will treat our classmates to dinner. How does that sound? （怎么样）

5.*A:* Why are you busy today? （为什么，因为）

   B: Because today is my mom's birthday.

6. I know my older brother's classmate, Little Zhang, but he doesn't know me.

Writing Practice

Write a note to your friend inviting him/her to have dinner with you tomorrow because it's your birthday.

LESSON 4 ▲ Hobbies
第四课 ▲ 爱好
Dì sì kè ▲ *Aìhào*

Part One

DIALOGUE I: TALKING ABOUT HOBBIES

I. Listening Comprehension

A. Textbook Dialogue I (True/False)

Quote the key sentence from the dialogue to support your answer.

( ) 1. Little Gao likes watching TV.

( ) 2. Little Bai does a lot of reading every weekend.

( ) 3. Little Bai not only likes to sing, but also dance.

( ) 4. Little Gao likes playing ball and listening to music on weekends.

( ) 5. Both Little Gao and Little Bai like to dance.

( ) 6. Little Bai is treating Little Gao to a movie.

B. Workbook Dialogue I (Multiple Choice)

( ) 1. What does the man like to do the most?

    a. go to a concert   b. play ball

    c. go to the movies   d. go dancing

( ) 2. If the man and the woman decide to do something together, they will most likely go to:

    a. a movie.   b. a concert.

    c. a dance.   d. a ball game.

C. Workbook Dialogue II (Multiple Choice)

( ) 1. The man invites the woman to:

    a. a dinner.   b. a movie.

    c. a dance.   d. a concert.

▼▼

( ) 2. The man gives the invitation because:

    a. the woman has invited him to a dinner before.

    b. the woman has invited him to a concert before.

    c. tomorrow is his birthday.

    d. tomorrow is her birthday.

( ) 3. Which of the following statements is true?

    a. The woman doesn't accept the invitation although she will not be busy tomorrow.

    b. The woman doesn't accept the invitation because she'll be busy tomorrow.

    c. The woman accepts the invitation although she'll be busy tomorrow.

    d. The woman accepts the invitation because she will not be busy tomorrow.

II. Speaking Exercises

A. Answer the questions in Chinese based on Textbook Dialogue I.

    1. What does Little Gao like to do on weekends?

    2. What does Little Bai like to do on weekends?

    3. What will Little Bai and Little Gao do tonight?

    4. Who is treating tonight?

    5. Who took whom to dinner yesterday?

B. Discuss your interests and hobbies with your friends, and then make an appointment with them based on your common interests.

III. Reading Comprehension

A. Match the phrases with the appropriate pictures.

1. 打球（　）　　2. 跳舞（　）　　3. 唱歌（　）

4. 听音乐（　）　　5. 看电视（　）

B. Read the passage and answer the questions. (True/False)

昨天是张律师的生日，他的同学王先生昨天晚上请他吃晚饭。因为王先生请张律师吃饭，所以张律师这个周末请王先生去看一个外国电影。

Questions:

（　）1. Yesterday was Lawyer Wang's birthday.

（　）2. Yesterday Lawyer Zhang didn't have dinner at home.

（　）3. Yesterday Mr. Wang and Lawyer Zhang went to see a foreign movie.

（　）4. Mr. Wang wants to take Lawyer Zhang to a movie because Lawyer Zhang took him out to dinner.

C. Read the following dialogue and answer the questions. (True/False)

> 昨天是小白的生日，所以他昨天晚上请王朋，李友和张英去跳舞。李友和张英都是女孩子。李友喜欢和王朋跳舞。小白请张英跳舞，可是张英不喜欢跳舞，所以昨天晚上小白和张英都没跳舞。

Questions:

( ) 1. Little Bai invited three friends yesterday evening to celebrate his birthday.

( ) 2. Wang Peng danced with both girls.

( ) 3. Li You preferred to dance with Wang Peng.

( ) 4. Xiao Bai danced for several hours.

D. Read the passage and answer the following questions in English.

> 我哥哥认识一个女孩子，她的名字叫李明英。李小姐今年二十岁，是大学生。我哥哥很喜欢她，常常请她吃晚饭。周末两个人喜欢去跳舞、看电影。可是李小姐的爸爸和妈妈不喜欢我哥哥。因为我哥哥今年三十八岁，有两个女儿。我也不喜欢他们两个人做男女朋友，因为李小姐是我的同学。

Questions:

1. What are the three things that we know about Miss Li?

2. What do the two lovebirds like to do on weekends?

3. What are the two reasons that Ms. Li's parents don't like their daughter dating the narrator's brother?

4. What's the narrator's attitude toward the relationship? Why does she feel this way?

IV. Writing & Grammar Exercises

Grammar and Usage

Use a word or phrase from each of the four following groups to make four sentences based on the Chinese word order of Subject + Time + Verb + Object.

Group 1: 美国饭，球，音乐，电影

Group 2: 明天晚上，这个周末，星期四，今天

Group 3: 去看，去听，去打，去吃

Group 4: 我们，我爸爸妈妈，小白和小高，王朋和李友

1. _____ 。

2. _____ 。

3. _____ 。

4. _____ 。

Translation

Translate the following sentences into Chinese using the words or phrases in parentheses.

1. Do you like to dance on weekends? (V + 不 + V)

2. I often invite my classmates to go to see foreign movies. (请 . . . 去 + V)

3. I like singing and listening to music. Sometimes I also like reading.

4. Because it was your treat yesterday, I'll take you to dinner tomorrow.
(因为 . . . 所以)

5. A: You like to sing, right?

   B: Yes, I sing very often.

6. Is tomorrow your younger brother's birthday (or not)? (V + 不 + V)

Writing Practice

List your hobbies in Chinese.

Part Two

DIALOGUE II: INVITING SOMEONE TO PLAY BALL

I. Listening Comprehension

A. Textbook Dialogue II (True/False)

Quote the key sentence from the dialogue to support your answer.

(   ) 1. Little Zhang does not like playing ball.

(   ) 2. Wang Peng wants to play ball this weekend.

(   ) 3. Little Zhang is very interested in movies.

(   ) 4. Wang Peng is going out to eat with Little Zhang.

(   ) 5. Little Zhang likes to sleep.

(   ) 6. In the end Wang Peng gives up the idea of going out with Little Zhang.

B. Workbook Dialogue III (True/False)

Quote the key sentence from the dialogue to support your answer.

(   ) 1. The woman doesn't like Chinese movies because her Chinese is not good enough.

(   ) 2. The woman prefers American movies over Chinese movies.

(   ) 3. The man invites the woman to an American movie at the end of the conversation.

C. Workbook Dialogue IV (True/False)

Quote the key sentence from the dialogue to support your answer.

(   ) 1. The woman invites the man to a concert.

(   ) 2. The man is interested in sports.

(   ) 3. The man invites the woman to go dancing.

D. Workbook Narrative (Multiple Choice)

( ) 1. The speaker probably spends most of his spare time:

    a. in movie theaters

    b. in concert halls.

    c. in front of a TV set

    d. in a library.

( ) 2. According to the speaker, Wang Peng loves:

    a. movies and TV.

    b. dancing and reading.

    c. dancing and music.

    d. reading only.

( ) 3. Which of the following statements is true about the speaker and Wang Peng?

    a. Wang Peng likes to read.

    b. The speaker likes to watch TV.

    c. Both the speaker and Wang Peng like to dance.

    d. Wang Peng and the speaker are classmates.

II. Speaking Exercises

A. Answer the questions in Chinese based on Textbook Dialogue II.

1. Did Wang Peng see Little Zhang yesterday? How do you know?

2. Does Little Zhang want to play ball? Why?

3. Does Little Zhang want to go to the movies? Why?

4. What does Little Zhang like to do?

5. What did Wang Peng finally decide to do this weekend?

B. Your partner is inviting you to do something. Keep rejecting the suggestions he/she makes and give reasons why you do not like those activities.

III. Reading Comprehension

A. Match the questions on the left with the appropriate replies on the right. Write down the letter in the parentheses.

( ) 1. 你叫什么名字？   　A. 我明天不忙。

( ) 2. 这是你弟弟吗？   　B. 今天晚上我很忙。

( ) 3. 你明天忙不忙？   　C. 我想看一个外国电影。

( ) 4. 你认识小张吗？   　D. 不，这是我哥哥。

( ) 5. 你喜欢听音乐吗？ 　E. 因为我喜欢吃美国饭。

( ) 6. 为什么你请我看电影？ F. 认识，他是我同学。

( ) 7. 为什么我们不吃中国饭？ G. 我叫王朋。

( ) 8. 我们去打球，好吗？ 　H. 我觉得听音乐没有意思。

( ) 9. 这个周末你做什么？ 　I. 我不想打球。

( ) 10. 今天晚上我去找你，　 J. 因为今天是你的生日。
　　　好吗？

B. Read the passage and answer the questions. (Multiple Choice)

小王和小李是同学。小王是中国人，他喜欢打球、看电视和看书。小李是美国人，她喜欢听音乐、唱歌和跳舞。他们都喜欢看电影，可是小王只喜欢看美国电影，小李觉得美国电影没有意思，她只喜欢看外国电影。她觉得中国电影很有意思。

( ) 1. What activities does Little Wang enjoy?

   a. watching TV and listening to music

   b. watching Chinese movies and dancing

   c. watching American movies and singing

   d. playing ball and reading

( ) 2. What does Little Li like to do?

    a. watch TV and listen to music

    b. watch Chinese movies and dance

    c. watch American movies and dance

    d. play ball and read

( ) 3. Which of the following statements is true?

    a. Little Wang and Little Li both like to watch TV.

    b. Little Wang is American and he likes American movies.

    c. Little Li is Chinese and she likes American movies.

    d. Little Wang and Little Li know each other.

( ) 4. If Little Wang and Little Li want to do something they are both interested in, where can they go together?

    a. a movie theater   b. a library

    c. a dancing party   d. none of the above

C. Read the following dialogue and answer the questions. (True/False)

小张：你喜欢看美国电影还是外国电影？

老李：我不喜欢看美国电影，也不喜欢看外国电影。

小张：你觉得中国音乐有意思还是美国音乐有意思？

老李：我觉得中国音乐和美国音乐都没有意思。

小张：你常常看中文书还是英文书？

老李：我不看中文书，也不看英文书。

小张：那你喜欢吃中国饭还是美国饭？

老李：中国饭和美国饭我都喜欢吃。

Questions:

( ) 1. This conversation most likely takes place in the United States.

( ) 2. Old Li does not like American movies, but likes foreign ones.

( ) 3. Old Li feels that both Chinese music and American music are boring.

( ) 4. When Old Li reads, the book must be in a language other than English or Chinese.

( ) 5. It seems Old Li does not like anything American or Chinese.

IV. Writing & Grammar Exercises

Grammar and Usage

A. Use "（没）有意思" *to complete the following dialogues.*

1.A: 你觉得昨天的电影＿＿＿＿＿＿＿＿吗？

B: 不，我觉得＿＿＿＿＿＿＿＿。

2.A: 你想去看中国电影吗？

B: 不想。我＿＿＿＿＿＿＿＿。

3.A: 你为什么不听中国音乐？

B: 因为＿＿＿＿＿＿＿＿。

4.A: 今天晚上的电视都很＿＿＿＿＿＿＿＿，
我们去唱歌，好不好？

B: 我不想去，我＿＿＿＿＿＿＿＿。

B. Use "因为...所以" *to answer the following questions.*

1.A: 小高为什么请小白看电影？

B:＿＿＿＿＿＿＿＿＿＿＿＿＿＿＿＿＿＿＿＿。

2.A: 小张为什么不想去打球？

B:＿＿＿＿＿＿＿＿＿＿＿＿＿＿＿＿＿＿＿＿。

3.A: 小张为什么不想去看电影？

B:＿＿＿＿＿＿＿＿＿＿＿＿＿＿＿＿＿＿＿＿＿。

C. Complete the following exchanges.

1.A: 你周末常常做什么？

B:＿＿＿＿＿＿＿＿＿＿＿＿＿＿＿＿＿＿＿＿＿。

2.A: 你喜欢看美国电影还是外国电影？

B:＿＿＿＿＿＿＿＿＿＿＿＿＿＿＿＿＿＿＿＿＿。

3.A: 星期一晚上的电影有意思还是星期六晚上的电影有意思？

B:＿＿＿＿＿＿＿＿＿＿＿＿＿＿＿＿＿＿＿＿＿。

4.A: 你今天晚上几点钟睡觉？

B:＿＿＿＿＿＿＿＿＿＿＿＿＿＿＿＿＿＿＿＿＿。

5.A: 你觉得看书有意思还是看电视有意思？

B:＿＿＿＿＿＿＿＿＿＿＿＿＿＿＿＿＿＿＿＿＿。

Translation

Translate the following sentences into Chinese using the words or phrases in parentheses.

1. Little Zhang, long time no see.

2. Do you feel like going to play ball this weekend? (V+不+V, 去+V)

3. I don't like reading. I only like eating, watching TV and sleeping. (只)

4. I think this foreign movie is very interesting. （有意思）

5. Then forget it. I'll go to bed. （去）

6. I am very busy today. I don't want to go to see the movie. （想）

7. I don't like foreign movies. I only like American movies. （只）

8. You don't feel like going to the movies. Then let's go dancing. How's that sound?

Writing Practice

Describe in detail what you did last weekend.

LESSON 5 ▲ Visiting Friends
第五课 ▲ 看朋友
Dì wǔ kè ▲ Kàn péngyou

Part One

DIALOGUE: VISITING A FRIEND'S HOME

I. Listening Comprehension

A. Textbook Dialogue (True/False)

Quote the key sentence from the dialogue to support your answer.

( ) 1. Wang Peng and Li You had met Little Gao's older sister before.

( ) 2. Li You was very happy to meet Little Gao's younger sister.

( ) 3. Li You thought that Little Gao's house was nice and big.

( ) 4. Little Gao's older sister works in a restaurant.

( ) 5. Li You did not drink beer.

( ) 6. Little Gao's sister gave Li You a cola.

( ) 7. Li You did not drink anything at Little Gao's house.

B. Workbook Dialogue I (True/False)

Quote the key sentence from the dialogue to support your answer.

( ) 1. The man and the woman run into each other in a library.

( ) 2. The man and the woman have never met each other before.

( ) 3. The man is looking for his younger brother.

C. Workbook Dialogue II (Multiple Choice)

( ) 1. The dialogue most likely occurs in:

    a. a car.   b. a house.

    c. a library.   d. a concert hall.

(   ) 2. Which of the following statements about the woman is true?

       a. She doesn't like TV in general but she likes what is on TV tonight.

       b. She doesn't like TV in general and she likes what is on TV tonight even less.

       c. She likes TV in general but she doesn't like what is on TV tonight.

       d. She likes TV in general and she particularly likes what is on TV tonight.

(   ) 3. What will they most likely do for the rest of the evening?

       a. watch TV   b. listen to American music

       c. read an American novel   d. listen to Chinese music

D. Workbook Dialogue III (Multiple Choice)

(   ) 1. Which of the following is the correct order of the woman's preferences?

       a. coffee, tea   b. beer, coffee

       c. coffee, beer   d. tea, coffee

(   ) 2. Which beverage does the man not have?

       a. tea   b. beer

       c. cola   d. coffee

(   ) 3. Which beverage does the woman finally get?

       a. tea   b. beer

       c. cola   d. coffee

II. Speaking Exercises

A. Answer the questions in Chinese based on the Textbook Dialogue.

1. Who went to Little Gao's house?

2. Did Wang Peng and Li You know Little Gao's older sister before?

3. What is Little Gao's older sister's name?

4. How is Little Gao's house?

5. Where does Little Gao's older sister work?

6. What did Wang Peng want to drink?

7. Why did Li You ask for a glass of water?

B. *This picture depicts a scene from Dialogue I of this lesson. Act it out with some of your classmates.*

C. *You are talking with a classmate's brother/sister for the first time. Find out if he/she is a student, where he/she works, and what his/her hobbies are.*

D. *You are visiting a friend's home. Compliment your friend on the home. Your friend offers you something to drink, so you ask for a glass of water.*

III. Reading Comprehension

A. *Read the following description carefully and match each of the names with the proper beverage by placing the letters in the appropriate parentheses.*

小高、小张和王朋都是同学，小高今年十九岁，小张今年二十岁，王朋今年二十一岁。小高不喜欢喝茶，小张不喝可乐，王朋喜欢喝咖啡、啤酒，可是不喜欢喝茶。

( )1. 小高　　　　　a. 茶

( )2. 小张　　　　　b. 啤酒

( )3. 王朋　　　　　c. 可乐

B. Read the following dialogue and answer the questions. (True/False)

（王亮和李乐都是美国学生。他们都学中文。）

王亮：你想喝点儿什么？

李乐：我要啤酒。

王亮：我不可以给你啤酒，因为你今年只有十九岁。

李乐：对，我今年十九岁，可是我为什么不可以喝啤酒？啤酒是 cola，对不对？

王亮：不对， cola 中文是可乐。

李乐：是吗？那请你给我一杯可乐吧。

王亮：好吧。

Questions:

(   ) 1. The two people know each other.

(   ) 2. The dialogue most likely occurred in Li Le's apartment.

(   ) 3. Li Le knew that he was too young to drink beer, but he asked for it anyway.

(   ) 4. Wang Liang's Chinese is probably better than Li Le's.

(   ) 5. Finally, Li Le got what he actually wanted.

IV. Writing & Grammar Exercises

Grammar and Usage

A. Answer the following questions.

1.A: 你常常在家看书还是在学校看书？

   B:_____。

2.A: 你爸爸妈妈在哪儿工作？

B: _____。

3.A: 你喜欢喝茶还是喜欢喝咖啡？

B: _____。

4.A: 你爸爸喜欢喝美国啤酒还是喜欢喝外国
啤酒？

B: _____。

B. *Use each group of words to make an interrogative sentence, a positive sentence, and a negative sentence.*

Example: 小高家/大

A. 小高家大不大？

B. 小高家很大。

C. 小高家不大。

1. 这个医生/好

A. _____?

B. _____。

C. _____。

2. 小白的妹妹/漂亮

A. _____?

B. _____。

C. _____。

3. 张律师/高兴

A. _____?

B. _____。

C. _____。

4. 那个电影/有意思

A. _____?

B. _____。

C. _____。

Translation

Translate the following sentences into Chinese, using the words or phrases in parentheses.

1. Let me introduce you. This is my classmate.

2. Very pleased to meet you. (认识)

3. Little Gao's home is very big and also very beautiful. (Adj.)

4.*A:* Where do you work? (在，哪儿)

B: I work at a school.

5. Would you like to have some coffee? (点儿)

▼▼▼

6. Would you like to drink cola or beer? (还是)

7.*A:* Please give me a cup of coffee.

   B: Sorry. We don't have coffee.

8. Come in quickly. Sit down please.

Writing Practice

List what you like to drink in Chinese.

Part Two

NARRATIVE: AT A FRIEND'S HOUSE

I. Listening Comprehension

A. Textbook Narrative (True/False)

Quote the key sentence from the dialogue to support your answer.

( ) 1. Little Gao's older sister works in a library.

( ) 2. Wang Peng had two glasses of beer at Little Gao's house.

( ) 3. Li You did not drink beer at Little Gao's house.

( ) 4. Wang Peng and Li You chatted and watched TV with Little Gao's sister last night.

( ) 5. Wang Peng and Li You left Little Gao's house at noon.

B. Workbook Narrative I (True/False)

Quote the key sentence from the dialogue to support your answer.

(   ) 1. The speaker thinks that Little Bai and Little Li are old friends.

(   ) 2. The three people are most likely at the speaker's place.

(   ) 3. Little Bai told Little Li that he works in the library.

C. Workbook Narrative II (Multiple Choice)

(   ) 1. Where did they spend last Saturday evening? They were:

     a. at Little Bai's place.   b. at Little Gao's place.

     c. at Little Li's place.   d. at Little Bai's brother's place.

(   ) 2. What did Little Bai's brother do at the party? He was:

     a. drinking.   b. watching TV.

     c. chatting.   d. dancing.

(   ) 3. Little Bai spent most of the evening:

     a. drinking and watching TV.   b. chatting and watching TV.

     c. drinking and chatting.   d. drinking, chatting and watching TV.

II. Speaking Exercises

A. Answer the questions in Chinese based on the Textbook Narrative.

1. Why did Wang Peng and Li You go to Little Gao's house?

2. Is Little Gao's older sister a teacher? Explain.

3. What did Wang Peng drink? How much?

4. What did Wang Peng and Li You do at Little Gao's house?

5. When did Wang Peng and Li You go home?

B. Explain in Chinese that you went to a friend's house last night. Your friend works at the school library. You chatted and watched TV together and did not return home until 11:30 p.m.

III. Reading Comprehension

A. Read the following note and answer the questions in English.

小张：

　　明天晚上七点半学校有一个中国电影，我们一起去看，好吗？请你晚上来找我。

　　　　　小高

　　　　　七月五日晚上九点半

1. Who wrote the note?

2. What time is the movie?

3. Where is the movie?

4. What date is the movie?

5. When was the note written?

B. *Read the passage and answer the questions. (Multiple Choice)*

> 昨天是小李的生日，小李请了小高、小张和王朋三个同学去她家吃饭。他们七点钟吃晚饭。小李的家很大，也很漂亮。小李的爸爸是老师，他很有意思。小李的妈妈是医生，昨天很忙，九点才回家吃晚饭。小李的哥哥和姐姐都不在家吃饭。王朋和小李的爸爸妈妈一起喝茶、聊天。小高、小张和小李一起喝可乐、看电视。小高、小张和王朋十一点才回家。

(　) 1. Where did Little Gao go last night?

　　a. Little Li's home　　　　　b. Little Zhang's home

　　c. Wang Peng's home　　　　d. His own home

(　) 2. Who was late for dinner last night?

　　a. Little Gao　　　　　　　b. Little Zhang

　　c. Little Li's father　　　　d. Little Li's mother

(　) 3. Which of the following statements is true?

　　a. Little Li's mother is a teacher.

　　b. Little Li's father is an interesting person.

　　c. Little Li's brother and sister were home last night.

　　d. Wang Peng talked with Little Li all evening.

C. *Read the passage and answer the questions. (True/False)*

> 今天小高去找他的同学小张，小张的妹妹也在家。可是小高不认识小张的妹妹。小张介绍了一下。小张的妹妹也是他们学校

的学生。她很漂亮，喜欢唱歌和看书。这个周末小高想请小张的妹妹去喝咖啡、看电影。

Questions:

(   ) 1. Little Gao has met Little Zhang's sister before.

(   ) 2. Little Gao and Little Zhang's sister attend the same school.

(   ) 3. Little Gao's sister likes to dance.

(   ) 4. Little Gao would like to invite Little Zhang and his sister to see a movie this weekend.

IV. Writing & Grammar Exercises

Grammar and Usage

A. Answer the following questions based on your own situation.

1. 你喜欢去同学家玩吗？为什么？

2. 你喜欢喝茶、可乐、咖啡还是啤酒？为什么？

3. 你喜欢在哪儿看书？

4. 你和你的同学常常一起做什么？

5. 昨天晚上你去没去朋友家玩儿？

B. *Change the following sentences from the positive to the negative.*

Example: A: 我昨天晚上看电视了。

→B: 我昨天晚上没(有)看电视。

1.A: 今天他打球了。

B: _____。

2.A: 我昨天晚上去小高家了。

B: _____。

3.A: 星期五是小高的生日，王朋喝啤酒了。

B: _____。

4.A: 星期三他去图书馆了。

B: _____。

C. *Answer the following questions in both the positive and the negative forms.*

Example: A: 你昨天晚上跳舞了吗？

→B1: 我昨天晚上跳舞了。

→B2: 我昨天晚上没(有)跳舞。

1.A: 小李昨天晚上喝茶了吗？

B1: _____。

B2: _____。

2.A: 你今天喝咖啡了吗？

B1: _____。

B2: _____。

3.*A:* 小白星期四回家了吗?

    B1: _____。

    B2: _____。

4.*A:* 星期六小高去朋友家玩了吗?

    B1: _____。

    B2: _____。

Translation

Translate the following sentences into Chinese, using the words or phrases in parentheses.

1. We got acquainted with Little Gao's older sister at the library. (在)

2. Last night they drank tea and chatted together. (聊天)

3. Last night Little Zhang drank four cups of coffee. (了, measure word)

4. Little Bai does not like beer. He only drank two glasses of cola.

5.*A:* Why did you get home as late as twelve? (才)

    B: Because I went to see a foreign movie.

6. Last night Wang Peng went to Li You's home for a visit. He met Li You's older sister.

7. Let's go home! (吧)

8. Let's eat dinner! (吧)

Writing Practice

A. *Describe a recent visit to your friend's house. Make sure that you mention what you did and what you drank.*

B. *Translate the following note into Chinese.*

> Yesterday evening I went to the library to read. In the library I met a classmate. We read together. I didn't go home until eleven o'clock.

LESSON 6 ▲ Making Appointments
第六课 ▲ 约时间
Dì liù kè ▲ *Yuē shíjiān*

Part One

DIALOGUE I: CALLING ONE'S TEACHER

I. Listening Comprehension

A. Textbook Dialogue I (Multiple Choice)

( ) 1. Why does Li You call Teacher Wang?

    a. Li You cannot come to school, because she is sick.

    b. Li You wants to ask some questions.

    c. Li You wants to know where Teacher Wang's office is.

    d. Li You wants to know where the meeting is.

( ) 2. What is Teacher Wang going to do this afternoon?

    a. teach two classes   b. go home early

    c. attend a meeting   d. go to a doctor's office

( ) 3. How many classes will Teacher Wang teach tomorrow morning?

    a. 1   b. 2

    c. 3   d. 4

( ) 4. What will Teacher Wang be doing at 3:30 tomorrow afternoon?

    a. attending a meeting   b. giving an exam

    c. working in his office   d. seeing a doctor

( ) 5. Where is Li You going to meet Teacher Wang?

    a. in Teacher Wang's office   b. in the classroom

    c. in the meeting room   d. in the library

( ) 6. When will Li You meet with Teacher Wang tomorrow?

    a. 9:00 a.m.   b. 10:30 a.m.

    c. 3:00 p.m.   d. 4:30 p.m.

B. *Workbook Dialogue I (True/False)*

Quote the key sentence from the dialogue to support your answer.

( ) 1. The woman in the dialogue is the man's sister.

( ) 2. The telephone call was originally not meant for the woman.

( ) 3. There is going to be a Chinese film tonight.

( ) 4. The woman will most likely stay home tonight.

C. *Workbook Dialogue II (Multiple Choice)*

( ) 1. Which of the following statements is true?

a. The woman invites the man to a dinner party at her home.

b. The woman invites the man to a dance at her home.

c. The woman hopes to go to the dinner party at the man's home.

d. The woman hopes to go to the dance at the man's home.

( ) 2. Why can't the man go?

a. He is giving a party.

b. He has to prepare for a test.

c. He has another dinner party to go to.

d. He has another dance to go to.

II. Speaking Exercises

A. *Answer the questions in Chinese based on Textbook Dialogue I.*

1. Why did Li You call Teacher Wang?

2. Will Teacher Wang be free this afternoon? Explain.

3. Will Teacher Wang be free tomorrow morning? Explain.

4. What will Teacher Wang do at three o'clock tomorrow afternoon?

5. When will Li You go to visit Teacher Wang?

6. Where will Teacher Wang and Li You meet?

B. *You are on the phone with your teacher. You would like to make an appointment with him/her. Your teacher happens to be busy at the time you suggest. Ask your teacher when he/she will be available. Decide on a time and place to meet.*

III. Reading Comprehension

A. Match the responses on the left with the expressions on the right. Write the appropriate letter in the parentheses.

( )1. 认识你们我也很高兴。

( )2. 不客气。

( )3. 再见。

( )4. 对不起，我不喝酒。

( )5. 对不起，小白不在。

( )6. 对不起，我今天下午要开会。

( )7. 对不起，我明天要考试。

( )8. 我是王朋。

A. 你是哪位？

B. 我们今天晚上去跳舞，好吗？

C. 喝点儿酒，怎么样？

D. 喂，请问小白在吗？

E. 认识你很高兴。

F. 谢谢。

G. 明天见。

H. 今天下午我来找你，好吗？

B. Read the following schedule and answer the questions. (True/False)

这是小王今天要做的事：

8:00	中文课
10:00	去白老师办公室
14:30	看王医生
16:00	开会
18:00	和小李吃饭
20:30	请小李喝咖啡
23:15	和小张去学校看电影

Questions:

( ) 1. 小王今天只有一节课。

( ) 2. 小王要和小李一起吃午饭。

( ) 3. 小王上午要找白老师。

( ) 4. 今天晚上小李要请小王喝咖啡。

( ) 5. 今天晚上小王要晚上十二点以后才回家。

C. Read the passage and answer the questions. (True/False)

李友是张老师的学生。今天上午李友给张老师打电话，因为她下个星期考试，想问张老师几个问题。可是张老师今天下午有课，没有时间见李友。张老师明天上午要开会，下午有两节课，三点半以后才有空。李友可以四点以后到办公室去找他。

Questions:

( )1. 今天上午张老师给李友打电话了。

( )2. 李友想请张老师给她考试。

( )3. 张老师今天下午不忙。

( )4. 张老师明天下午两点半要上课。

( )5. 李友明天四点钟以后可以去问张老师几个问题。

D. Read the following dialogue and answer the questions.

(李友给王朋打电话。李友问了王朋几个问题。)

王朋：还有别的问题吗？

李友：我还有一个问题。

王朋：你问吧。

李友：你明天下午有空吗？

王朋：我明天下午要开会。

李友：明天晚上呢？

王朋：我明天晚上也没有时间。我想请一位女孩子去听音乐。

李友：那算了。

王朋：你认识那个女孩子。

李友：是吗？她叫什么名字？

王朋：她姓李，叫李友。

Questions:

(True/False)

(　) 1. Li You's schedule for tomorrow seems quite flexible.

(　) 2. Wang Peng hopes to see Li You tomorrow.

(　) 3. Li You does not know the girl Wang Peng mentioned.

(Multiple Choice)

(　) 4. The conversation mostly likely took place:

    a. in a movie theater.

    b. at a concert.

    c. in a dorm.

(　) 5. On hearing of Wang Peng's plan for tomorrow evening, Li You must be:

    a. first disappointed and then very happy.

    b. first very happy and then disappointed.

    c. neither happy nor disappointed.

IV. Writing & Grammar Exercises

Grammar and Usage

A. Fill in the blanks with appropriate measure words.

1. 两 _____ 问题

2. 您是哪 _____？

3. 三 _____ 课

4. 四 _____ 茶 (cup)

5. 五 _____ 啤酒 (bottle)

B. Use 要是 *to answer the following questions.*

1. 要是你明天没课，你想做什么？

2. 要是今天你们的老师请你们吃饭，你想吃美国饭还是吃中国饭？

3. 要是你明天考试，你想在图书馆还是在家看书？

4. 要是你有空，你想去看电影还是想去打球？

Translation

Translate the following sentences into Chinese, using the words or phrases in parentheses.

1. This morning my teacher called me. (给，了)

2. Teacher, are you free this weekend? I'd like to invite you to dinner. (有时间，请)

3. When will you be free this weekend? (有空儿)

4. This afternoon I went to look for Teacher Zhang, but he wasn't in his office. (可是，在)

5. Tomorrow afternoon I have two classes. I won't be free until after three thirty. (以后，才)

6. This afternoon I have to give an exam to the first-year class. (要)

7. If it's convenient for you, I will go to your office at 4:00 p.m. Is that all right? (要是，去)

8. Don't go to his office. (别)

9. Buy you dinner? No problem!

10.*A:* Hello. Is Little Bai there?

B: This is he. Who is this?

Writing Practice

List the things that you need to do today. Don't forget to include the times.

Part Two

DIALOGUE II: CALLING A FRIEND FOR HELP

I. Listening Comprehension

A. Textbook Dialogue II (True/False)

Quote the key sentence from the dialogue to support your answer.

( ) 1. Li You is returning Wang Peng's phone call.

( ) 2. Li You has an examination next week.

( ) 3. Li You is asking Wang Peng to practice Chinese with her.

( ) 4. Wang Peng is inviting Li You to have coffee.

( ) 5. Wang Peng is going to have dinner with Li You this evening.

( ) 6. Wang Peng does not know exactly when he is going to call Li You.

B. Listen to Dialogue II very carefully to see if you can locate the section depicted by the illustration below.

C. *Workbook Dialogue III (True/False)*

Quote the key sentence from the dialogue to support your answer.

( ) 1. Tomorrow will be Friday.

( ) 2. Li You cannot go for the dinner tomorrow because she will be busy.

( ) 3. Li You will be practicing Chinese this evening.

( ) 4. Wang Peng promises to help Li You with her Chinese tomorrow at 6:00 p.m.

D. *Workbook Dialogue IV (True/False)*

Quote the key sentence from the dialogue to support your answer.

( ) 1. Wang Peng cannot help Li You practice Chinese because he has classes tomorrow afternoon.

( ) 2. Wang Peng asks Miss Bai to help Li You with her Chinese.

( ) 3. Miss Bai and Li You will meet at 2:00 p.m. tomorrow in the library.

II. Speaking Exercises

A. *Answer the questions in Chinese based on Textbook Dialogue II.*

1. Why did Li You call Wang Peng? Please explain.

2. Why did Wang Peng ask Li You to invite him for coffee?

3. What will Wang Peng do tonight?

4. When will Wang Peng call Li You?

5. Will Li You go to see a movie tonight? Please explain.

B. *You are calling a friend to ask for a favor and you promise to treat him/her to something in return. You would like to meet him/her tonight, but he/she is going to see a movie and does not know when he/she will be back. He/she promises that he/she will give you a call when he/she comes back.*

C. *You are calling a friend to ask a favor. Your friend is willing to help you. Decide on a time and place to meet, and promise that you will take your friend out to a foreign movie.*

III. Reading Comprehension

A. Read this note and answer the following questions. (Multiple Choice)

小高：

　　小张下午打电话给你了。他想请你
星期四下午帮他练习中文，不知道你
有没有空。回来以后给他打电话，他
的电话是 324-6597。

　　　　　　　　　　姐姐

　　　　三月八号(星期二)下午三点

Questions:

( ) 1. Who wrote the note?

　　a. 小高。　　　　　　b. 小张。

　　c. 小高的姐姐。　　d. 小张的姐姐。

( ) 2. Which of the following is true?

　　a. 小张星期四下午给小高打了一个电
　　　话。
　　b. 小高知道星期四下午要帮小张练习说
　　　中文。
　　c. 小高的姐姐请小高回来以后给小张打
　　　电话。
　　d. 小高的姐姐给小张打了一个电话。

( ) 3. Which of the following is true?

　　a. 明天是星期四。
　　b. 明天是三月九号。

c.三月八号是星期四。

d.三月十号是星期二。

B. Authentic Materials

Below is a page of Little Gao's appointment book. Take a look at the things that he plans to do this week and answer the following questions in English.

August 5 - 7

5 MONDAY

-九点半去周老师的办公室

-下午三点去图书馆

-跟王朋练习说中文

6 TUESDAY

-中文考试

7 WEDNESDAY

-下午四点请王朋

-喝咖啡

8 - 11 August

THURSDAY 8

-姐姐生日

-打电话回家

FRIDAY 9

-下午五点和小白去

-看电影

10 SATURDAY   SUNDAY 11

-回家吃午饭

Questions:

1. 他星期天在哪儿吃饭？

2. 他什么时候考中文？

3. 他和王朋在哪儿练习中文？

4. 他姐姐的生日是几月几号？

5. 他星期五下午有什么事？

6. 他请谁喝咖啡？

7. 他们星期几喝咖啡？

8. 他们几点钟喝咖啡？

9. 他星期天中午在哪儿？

C. Read the passage and answer the questions. (True/False)

小张今天很忙，上午有四节课，中午和同学一起吃饭，下午在图书馆看书，和小李练习中文，晚上到小白的学校去看电影，十一点才回家。因为明天他有两个考试，所以今天晚上他没有时间睡觉。

Questions:

( ) 1. 小张今天没有时间吃午饭。

( ) 2. 小张今天下午没有课。

( ) 3. 小张今天和小李在图书馆练习中文。

( ) 4. 小白不是小张学校的学生。

( ) 5. 今天晚上十点半小张不在家。

( ) 6. 因为小张要看电影，所以他今天晚上
没有时间睡觉。

D. Read the following note and answer the questions.

王朋：

李友今天上午十点钟给你打电话了。
她昨天晚上才知道星期五下午有中文考
试，所以她今天晚上不和你去听音乐。
要是你有空，她想今天下午请你帮她练
习中文，她考试以后请你看电影。你回
来以后给她打一个电话吧。

小高

十二点半

Questions:

(True/False)

( ) 1. Xiao Gao is most likely Wang Peng's roommate.

( ) 2. Wang Peng was not in at 10:00 a.m. but was back around 12:25 p.m.

( ) 3. At 4:00 p.m. yesterday Li You still planned to go to the concert.

( ) 4. We do not know when Wang Peng will call Li You back.

( ) 5. Li You was certain that Wang Peng would be available this afternoon.

(Multiple Choice)

( ) 6. Which of the statements is true?

    a. Li You had been told last Friday that there would be an exam last night.

    b. Li You was told yesterday evening that there would be an exam on Friday.

    c. Li You was told that yesterday evening's exam was postponed till Friday.

( ) 7. Li You hopes to take Wang Peng to a movie this:

    a. Wednesday evening.

    b. Thursday evening.

    c. Friday evening.

IV. Writing & Grammar Exercises

Grammar and Usage

A. Answer the following questions using the words in parentheses and 得 *(děi).*

Example: 为什么今天晚上你不去跳舞？（看书）

→因为今天晚上我得看书。

1. 为什么你不睡觉？（等我妹妹的电话）

2. 为什么你不看电视？（练习说中文）

3. 为什么你今天下午没有空儿？（开会）

B. *Answer the following questions.*

1. 谁常常给你打电话？

2. 你是大学几年级的学生？

3. 你星期四几点钟有中文课？

4. 你星期一有几节课？

5. 你明天有没有考试？

6. 你知道不知道你的中文老师叫什么名字？

7. 你喜欢和同学一起去跳舞吗？

C. *Complete the following sentences with* 但是.

1. 我想今天下午去找王老师，

_____ 。

2. 我想这个周末去看电影，

_____ 。

3. 我想请我的同学帮忙，

_____ 。

4. 我想给你打电话，

_____ 。

D. Rearrange the following Chinese words into sentences, using the English sentences as clues.

1. 四点/我/办公室/电话/在/明天/等/以后/下
午/你的

(I will be waiting for your phone call in the office after 4:00 p.m. tomorrow.)

2. 有人/不知道/请我/晚上/回来/什么/时候/
今天/吃晚饭

(Someone is taking me out for dinner this evening. I don't know when I will
be back.)

3. 您/回来/给我/方便/请/以后/打/要是/电话

(If it is convenient for you, please give me a call after you come back.)

Translation

Translate the following sentences into Chinese, using the words or phrases in
parentheses.

1. Because I need to take a Chinese exam next Thursday, I'd like to ask Wang
Peng to help me practice speaking Chinese this weekend.
（因为...所以，请，帮）

2. I'll wait for you, but you have to treat me to a movie. （但是，得）

3. I'll go look for you after I get back. （以后）

4. I'll wait for your call after I get back home. （以后，等）

5. Sorry! I will not be free next week.

Writing Practice

A. Write a note to your Chinese friend to see if he/she can practice Chinese with you tomorrow evening. Promise him/her that you will buy him/her a cup of coffee afterwards.

B. Write a description of Little Wang's life.

Little Wang is often busy. He likes to go to the movies, but he has no time for that; he also likes to listen to music, but he has no time for that, either. Tomorrow he will be free. He will take Miss Bai out to dinner tomorrow evening. He doesn't know when she will be back home tomorrow afternoon, but he will wait for her to call.

LESSON 7 ▲ Studying Chinese
第七课 ▲ 学中文
Dì qī kè ▲ Xué Zhōngwén

Part One

DIALOGUE I: ASKING ABOUT AN EXAMINATION

I. Listening Comprehension

A. Textbook Dialogue I (True/False)

Quote the key sentence from the dialogue to support your answer.

(   ) 1. Li You didn't do very well on her test last week.

(   ) 2. Wang Peng writes Chinese well, but very slowly.

(   ) 3. Wang Peng didn't want to teach Li You how to write Chinese characters.

(   ) 4. Li You is prepared for tomorrow's lesson.

(   ) 5. The Chinese characters in Lesson Seven are very easy.

(   ) 6. Li You has no problems with Lesson Seven's grammar.

B. Workbook Narrative (True/False)

Quote the key sentence from the dialogue to support your answer.

(   ) 1. Mr. Li is an American.

(   ) 2. Mr. Li likes studying Chinese, but not English.

(   ) 3. Mr. Li feels that English grammar is not too difficult, but Chinese grammar is hard.

(   ) 4. Mr. Li is having a hard time learning Chinese characters.

C. Workbook Dialogue I (True/False)

(Little Wang is talking to Little Bai.)

(   ) 1. Little Bai didn't do very well on the Chinese test last week.

(   ) 2. Little Wang is not willing to practice Chinese with Little Bai.

(   ) 3. Little Bai is very good at Chinese characters.

(   ) 4. Little Wang can help Little Bai with both speaking and writing.

II. Speaking Exercises

A. Answer the questions in Chinese based on Textbook Dialogue I.

1. How did Li You do on last week's test, and why?

2. Why does Wang Peng offer to help Li You with her writing of Chinese characters?

3. Who can write Chinese characters fast?

4. Which lesson will Li You study tomorrow?

5. How does Li You feel about the grammar, vocabulary and characters in the lesson she has prepared?

6. What will Wang Peng and Li You do tonight?

B. Discuss the results of the recent Chinese tests you have taken with your friend. Comment on how you did on grammar, vocabulary and Chinese characters.

C. Make up a story based on the picture below. Try to use the new words and sentence structures that you have learned in this lesson.

III. Reading Comprehension

A. Read the note and answer the questions. (True/False)

小王：

你好！我上个星期有个中文考试，我考得不太好，老师说我汉字写得不错，可是太慢。中文语法也有一点儿难，我不太懂。这个周末你有时间吗？我想请你帮助我复习中文。我们一起练习说中文，好吗？

小白

十月二十七日

Questions:

( )1. 小白上个星期考试考得不错。

( )2. 老师说小白写汉字写得很好，也很快。

( )3. 小白觉得中文语法很容易，她都懂。

( )4. 小白要小王帮助她复习中文。

B. Read the passage and answer the questions. (True/False)

昨天是小高的生日，李友和王朋都到小高家去了。他们一起喝啤酒，听音乐，唱歌，晚上十二点才回家，一点钟才睡觉。因为李友没有复习中文，所以今天考试考得不好。

Questions:

( ) 1. 李友和王朋都是小高的朋友。

( ) 2. 昨天晚上十点钟李友、王朋和小高都不在家。

( ) 3. 王朋昨天晚上喝啤酒了，可是李友没有喝。

( ) 4. 李友昨天没有时间复习中文。

( ) 5. 王朋昨天晚上睡觉睡得很晚。

( ) 6. 李友觉得今天的考试很容易。

IV. Writing & Grammar Exercises

Grammar and Usage

A. Answer the following questions.

　　Example: A: 你昨天睡觉睡得晚吗？

　　　　　　B: 我睡觉睡得很晚。

1.A: 你写字写得快吗？

　　B: _____。

2.A: 你妹妹唱歌唱得好吗？

　　B: _____。

3.A: 你哥哥打球打得好吗？

　　B: _____。

4.A: 她跳舞跳得怎么样？

　　B: _____。

5.A: 你说中文说得怎么样？

　　B: _____。

B. Fill in the blanks based on the hints given in parentheses.

我和我的姐姐 _____(both) 喜欢听 _____
(music)。我们 _____ (often) _____ (together) 听。
我们 _____ (also) 喜欢 _____ (study) 中文。
_____ (however)，中国人说中文说得 _____
(too) 快。我 _____ (feel) 语法也 _____ (a bit)
难。

▼▼▼▼▼▼▼▼▼▼▼▼▼▼▼▼▼▼▼▼▼▼▼▼▼▼▼▼▼▼▼▼▼

C. Complete the sentences with 才 *or* 就:

Example: 我们三点开会，可是<u>李小姐四点才</u>
<u>来</u>。（才）

我们三点开会，可是<u>李小姐两点就来</u>
<u>了</u>。（就）

1. 我们八点钟有中文课，可是

_____。（才）

2. 小王今天下午没有课，所以

_____。（就）

3. 我昨天晚上去朋友家玩儿，

_____。（才）

4. 她妈妈说明天来，可是

_____。（就）

5. 因为我今天有考试，所以我昨天晚上
复习生词，

_____。（才）

6. 我哥哥说今天晚上给我打电话，可是

_____。（就）

D. Make sentences using the given words and 得.

Example: 说中文/好

→ 他说中文说得很好。

▼▼

1. 写字/好

2. 说英文/快

3. 打球/不好

4. 学汉字/不太快

5. 喝啤酒/多

Translation

Translate the following sentences into Chinese, using the words or phrases in parentheses.

1. The teacher writes Chinese characters very well.

2. She feels that Chinese grammar is a little bit hard. （有一点儿）

3. Because I am very busy, I will not go to the library until tomorrow afternoon. （就/才） yin wei wo hen mang, wo mingtian xia wa cai qu tu shuguan.

4. I went to the school (as early as) at seven o'clock today.
wo jintian zao shang qi dian jiu qu xue xiao le.

5. You write characters too slowly. (太...了)

ni zi xie de tai man le.

6. I feel that the text of Lesson Six is a little difficult.

wo jue de di qi liu ke de ne wen you yi dicr yi dian nan.

7. Teach me how to write Chinese characters, OK?

Jiao wo zenme xie zhong guo zi, hao bna?

8. Please help me review Lesson Six, OK?

cibs ni bang zhu wo fu xie di liu ke, hao ma?

Writing Practice

Write a paragraph (5–10 sentences) describing your experience learning Chinese.

Part Two

DIALOGUE II: PREPARING FOR A CHINESE CLASS

I. Listening Comprehension

A. Textbook Dialogue II (True/False)

Quote the key sentence from the dialogue to support your answer.

( ) 1. Little Bai is always late.

( ) 2. Little Bai didn't go to bed until after midnight last night.

( ) 3. Li You went to bed very late, because she was studying Chinese.

( ) 4. Little Bai has a very good Chinese friend.

( ) 5. Li You recited the lesson well, because she listened to the recording the night before.

( ) 6. Li You has a very handsome Chinese friend according to Little Bai.

B. Workbook Dialogue II (True/False)

Quote the key sentence from the dialogue to support your answer.

(Little Li is talking to Little Zhang.)

( ) 1. Little Zhang usually comes early.

( ) 2. Little Zhang previewed Lesson Eight.

( ) 3. Little Zhang went to bed early because he didn't have homework last night.

( ) 4. Little Zhang usually goes to bed around 9:00 p.m.

II. Speaking Exercises

A. Answer the questions in Chinese based on Textbook Dialogue II.

1. Why did Little Bai come so late today?

2. Why was Li You able to go to bed early last night?

3. Why did Little Bai say that it is nice to have a Chinese friend?

4. Which lesson is the class studying today?

5. Who did not listen to the recording last night?

6. How did Little Bai describe Li You's friend?

B. *Find out why your friend is late or early for the class, and how he/she prepares for each new lesson.*

III. Reading Comprehension

A. *Read Li You's schedule for today and answer the questions. (True/False)*

上午	八点半	预习生词
	九点一刻	听录音
	十点	上中文课
中午	十二点	吃午饭
下午	一点	睡午觉
	两点	复习中文
晚上	六点	吃晚饭
	八点	做功课

Questions:

( ) 1. 李友今天没有课。

( ) 2. 李友上午预习生词。

( ) 3. 李友下午听录音。

( ) 4. 李友不吃午饭，只吃晚饭。

( ) 5. 李友复习中文以后睡午觉。

( ) 6. 李友吃晚饭以后做功课。

B. Read the passage and answer the questions. (True/False)

今天上午，小李预习了第六课。第六课的语法有点儿难，生词也很多。下午她要去老师的办公室问问题。她觉得学中文很有意思。说中国话不太难，可是汉字有一点儿难。

Questions:

（　）1. 小李觉得第六课不太容易。

（　）2. 今天下午小李的老师在办公室。

（　）3. 小李想今天下午给老师打电话。

（　）4. 小李很喜欢学中文。

（　）5. 小李觉得学汉字不容易。

IV. Writing & Grammar Exercises

Grammar and Usage

A. Complete the sentences or fill in sentences in the dialogues using 因为 *or* 所以.

1. 因为昨天晚上没有功课，

   _____ 。

2. 因为你有中国朋友帮助你复习，

   _____ 。

3. A: 你怎么没去看电影？

   B: _____ 。

4. A: 你为什么请他喝咖啡？

   B: _____ 。

5. _____ ，

   所以他很晚才睡觉。

B. Fill in the blanks with 真 *or* 太.

1. 你这张照片 _____ 漂亮。

2. 那个学校 _____ 大了。

3. 今天的功课 _____ 多了。

4. 这个工作 _____ 有意思。

5. 第六课的生词 _____ 多。

6. 李友的妈妈 _____ 客气了。

Translation

Translate the following sentences into Chinese, using the words or phrases in parentheses.

1. Last night I was not back home until ten o'clock. (就/才)

2. How come your younger brother didn't go to the movie on Wednesday?

3. His older sister sings really well. (真)

4. *A:* How come you are so happy today? (怎么)

   B: Because I did very well on the test. (得)

5. I previewed Lesson Seven. The grammar is easy.

6. Your pen is really beautiful.

7. Good morning, everybody. Let's begin the lesson. Please read the text.

8. Your boyfriend is really handsome!

9. I listened to the tape. But I did not understand it.

Writing Practice

Translate the following paragraph into Chinese.

My younger sister did not learn Chinese well. She didn't like listening to recordings and didn't practice speaking, so she did not speak well. She didn't like studying grammar or writing characters. That was why she didn't do well on examinations. But after she met a Chinese friend, she and her friend often practice speaking Chinese in the library. Now, she likes listening to tapes and writing characters.

LESSON 8 ▲ School Life
第八课 ▲ 学校生活
Dì bā kè ▲ *Xuéxiào shēnghuó*

Part One

A DIARY: A TYPICAL SCHOOL DAY

I. Listening Comprehension

A. A Diary (Multiple Choice)

(   ) 1. Which day of the week is August 10?

    a. Monday   b. Tuesday   c. Wednesday   d. Thursday

(   ) 2. What did Li You do this morning before breakfast?

    a. She took a bath.

    b. She listened to the recording.

    c. She read the newspaper.

    d. She talked to her friend on the phone.

(   ) 3. What time did Li You go to class this morning?

    a. 7:30   b. 8:00   c. 8:30   d. 9:00

(   ) 4. What did Li You NOT do in her Chinese class?

    a. take a test   b. practice pronunciation

    c. learn vocabulary   d. study grammar

(   ) 5. Where did Li You have lunch today?

    a. at a Chinese restaurant   b. in the school's dining hall

    c. at home   d. at her friend's house

(   ) 6. What was Li You doing around 4:30 p.m.?

    a. practicing Chinese   b. reading a newspaper

    c. playing ball   d. drinking coffee

(   ) 7. What time did Li You eat her dinner?

    a. 5:45   b. 6:00   c. 6:30   d. 7:30

( ) 8. Li You went to Little Bai's dorm to:

     a. eat dinner.   b. read the newspaper.

     c. chat.   d. study.

( ) 9. What time did Li You return home?

     a. 7:30   b. 8:30   c. 9:30   d. 10:30

( ) 10. What did Li You do before she went to bed?

     a. visited Little Bai   b. did her homework

     c. called Wang Peng   d. prepared for her test

B. Use the numbers 1-3 to put the pictures in the correct sequence based on the information given in A Diary.

     ( )   ( )   ( )

C. Workbook Dialogue (True/False)

Quote the key sentence from the dialogue to support your answer.

( ) 1. Li You is going to Teacher Zhang's office at 4:00 p.m. today.

( ) 2. Wang Peng will be attending a class at 2:30 p.m. today.

( ) 3. Li You plans to read newspapers in the library this evening.

( ) 4. Li You and Wang Peng will see each other in the library this evening.

II. Speaking Exercises

A. Answer the questions in Chinese based on A Diary.

1. When was the diary entry written?

2. What time did Li You get up on that day?

3. What did Li You do before 9:00 a.m. on that day?

4. What did Li You do in her Chinese class on that day?

5. Did Li You like her computer class? Why?

▼▼▼

6. What did Li You do during the lunch hour?

7. What did Li You do that afternoon?

8. Describe what Li You did that evening.

B. Call your Chinese friend and describe to him/her what you did yesterday at school.

C. Tell a story based on the pictures below. Don't forget to mention the times.

III. Reading Comprehension

A. Answer the questions about A Diary *in English or in Chinese.*

1. 这是几月几号的日记?

2. 李友早上开始听录音以前做什么事?

3. 今天上午李友有几节课? 是什么课?

4. 李友中午在哪儿吃饭？

5. 李友下午在图书馆做什么？

6. 李友跟谁一起打球？

7. 李友为什么去找小白？

8. 李友告诉王朋什么事？

B. Read the following schedule and answer the questions. (True/False)

小张今天要做的事：	
8:00	复习第七课生词、语法
9:00	上电脑课
10:00	去王老师办公室练习发音
14:30	去图书馆看报
16:00	去打球
18:00	去宿舍餐厅吃饭
20:15	给小李打电话，请他一起练习中文
21:30	给爸爸妈妈打电话

Questions:

( ) 1. 小张今天只有一节课。

( ) 2. 小张跟小白一起吃午饭。

( ) 3. 小张上午去见王老师。

( ) 4. 小张去小李家练习中文。

( ) 5. 小张吃晚饭以前去打球。

( ) 6. 小张去图书馆以后去找王老师。

( ) 7. 小张睡觉以前给爸爸妈妈打电话。

( ) 8. 小张练习中文以后才吃饭。

C. Read the passage and answer the questions. (True/False)

小白以前常常跟朋友一起打球，聊天，看电视，不做功课。可是因为他下星期要考试，所以这个星期他不打球，不看电视，也不找朋友聊天，一个人到图书馆去看书。他很早就起床，很晚才睡觉，所以他上课的时候常常想睡觉。

Questions:

( ) 1. 小白以前常常跟朋友一边做功课，一边聊天。

( ) 2. 小白常常跟朋友到图书馆去看书。

( ) 3. 小白这个星期不打球，也不看电视，可是找朋友聊天儿。

( ) 4. 小白觉得上课没有意思，所以他上课
的时候常常想睡觉。

( ) 5. 这个星期小白睡觉睡得很早。

IV. Writing & Grammar Exercises

Grammar and Usage

A. Complete the following dialogues. Each sentence should contain a double-object structure.

Example: A: 他教<u>谁</u>中文？

→ 他教<u>他弟弟中文</u>。

1. A: 王老师教学生_____？
   B: 王老师教_____。

2. A: 小高给_____一本书？
   B: 小高给_____。

3. A: 李友问谁_____？
   B: 李友问_____。

4. A: 高小音给_____一杯茶？
   B: 高小音给_____。

5. A: 你告诉王朋_____了？
   B: 我告诉王朋_____。

B. Follow the model and rewrite the sentences.

Example: 他吃饭的时候听音乐。

→ 他一边吃饭一边听音乐。

1. 他听音乐的时候看报。

2. 我们吃饭的时候练习说中文。

3. 我的朋友喜欢写字的时候听音乐。

4. 张小姐吃饭的时候看电视。

Translation

Translate the following sentences into Chinese, using the words or phrases in parentheses.

1. My older sister taught me to sing, and I taught her to dance.

2. She wrote her Chinese diary very well. (complement with 得)

3.*A*: I'd like to go to the dining hall to have lunch. (到...去 + v)

B: I had lunch as early as eleven. (就) I want to go to the library to read the newspapers. (到...去 + V)

4. My older brother takes a shower right after getting up. (以后，就)

5. Li You dances very well, but she does not dance much. (complement with 得，不常)

6. I go to class after breakfast. (以后)

7. When I went to Little Li's dorm yesterday morning, she was chatting with Little Bai. (...的时候，...正在...)

8. I told my teacher already.

Writing Practice

Write a diary entry in Chinese about your school life.

Part Two

A LETTER: TALKING ABOUT STUDYING CHINESE

I. Listening Comprehension

A. A Letter (True/False)

Quote the key sentence from the dialogue to support your answer.

( ) 1. This is a letter from Yiwen to Miss Zhang.

( ) 2. Yiwen's major is Chinese.

( ) 3. Yiwen does not like her Chinese class at all.

( ) 4. Yiwen's Chinese friend speaks very clearly.

( ) 5. Yiwen is learning Chinese fast, because she has a Chinese friend.

( ) 6. Yiwen would like Miss Zhang to attend her school concert.

B. Workbook Narrative

( ) 1. Wang Peng went to the library to help Li You with her Chinese.

( ) 2. Wang Peng did not go to play ball this afternoon until he had finished his homework.

( ) 3. Li You went to a movie with Wang Peng this evening.

( ) 4. Li You has a Chinese class tomorrow.

II. Speaking Exercises

A. Answer the questions in Chinese based on A Letter.

1. Why is Yiwen so busy this semester?

2. Describe Yiwen's Chinese class.

3. Is Yiwen making progress in her Chinese class? Why?

4. Why did Yiwen ask Miss Zhang if she likes music?

5. Do you think Yiwen has confidence in her Chinese? Why?

B. Describe your Chinese class in detail to your friend. Make sure to comment on how you feel about pronunciation, grammar, vocabulary, and Chinese characters.

C. *Interview your classmate and find out:*

    1. when he/she gets up in the morning;

    2. whether he/she takes a shower in the morning after getting up or before
       going to bed at night;

    3. whether he/she prefers to have lunch at home or at school;

    4. what time he/she goes to school;

    5. what time he/she has his/her lunches and dinners;

    6. what time he/she returns home after school;

    7. what time he/she goes to bed.

III. Reading Comprehension

A. *Answer the questions about* A Letter.

1. 写信的人叫什么名字？

2. 你觉得意文喜欢她的中文课吗？为什么？

3. 上中文课的时候意文能说英文吗？

4. 意文常常跟谁一起练习说中文？

5. 意文为什么给张小姐写信？

B. Read the note and answer the questions. (True/False)

小王：

今天晚上七点半学校有一个很好的音乐会，我想请你跟我一起去。请你回来以后给我打电话。我的电话是：八五七九五六三。

小谢

七月五日下午四点半

Questions:

( ) 1. Little Xie plans to call Little Wang this evening at 7:30.

( ) 2. At 4:30 Little Wang was most likely not home.

( ) 3. Little Xie is certain that Little Wang knows her phone number.

( ) 4. Little Xie is hoping to spend the evening with Little Wang.

C. Read the passage and answer the questions. (True/False)

小张今天很忙，上午除了有三节课以外，还有一个电脑考试。中午跟朋友一起吃饭，下午在图书馆看书，做功课，晚上在电脑室工作，十点钟回家吃晚饭。晚饭以后，他一边看电视，一边预习明天的功课，十二点半才睡觉。

Questions:

( ) 1. 小张上午没空。

（　）2. 小张下午不在家，在图书馆看报。

（　）3. 小张晚上很晚才吃饭。

（　）4. 小张晚上在电脑室预习明天的功课。

（　）5. 小张一边听音乐，一边看书。

IV. Writing & Grammar Exercises

Grammar and Usage

A.. *Following the model, combine the sentences in each group into one that contains the* "除了 . . . 以外，还" *structure.*

Example: 我学中文。我也学日文。

→ 除了中文以外，我还学日文。

1. 我喜欢听音乐。我也喜欢跳舞。

chu le xi huen ting yin yue yi wei, wo hai xi huen tiao wu.

2. 他常常打球。他也常常看电影。

ta ~~chang chang~~ chu le chang chang da qiu yi wei, ye chang chan tian dian ing.

3. 今天晚上我想写信。今天晚上我也想给我
妈妈打电话。

wo jin tian wen shang chu le xiang xie xin yi wei,
hai xiang gei wo ma ma da dian hua.

4. 明天我有一节电脑课。明天我也有两节英
文课。

wo ming tian chu le yu yi jie dian nao ke yi wei,
hai you liang jie ying wen ke.

5. 他预习了生词。他也预习了课文。

chu le yu xi le sheng ci, ta hai yu xi le ke wen
yi wai

6. 我喜欢打球。我也喜欢找朋友聊天。

chu le xi huan da qiu yi wai, hai xi huan zhao peng you liao tian.

B. Answer the questions.

1. 除了中文课以外，你还有什么课？

wo hai you Math ne religion kic.

2. 你常常跟谁一起去看电影？

wo bu chang qu kan dian ying. chang chang ziji kan dian ying

3. 你平常睡觉以前做什么？

4. 你平常起床以后做什么？

Translation

Translate the following sentences into Chinese, using the words or phrases in parentheses.

1. At the beginning, I was not used to listening to the recording while having breakfast at the same time.

2. This morning the teacher gave us a lot of homework.

3. I hope that you can go to the concert with me.

4. We often speak Chinese and play ball at the same time. (一边 . . . 一边 . . .)

5. In addition to pronunciation, Mr. Wang also teaches us grammar. (除了 . . . 以外，也 . . .)

6. Wang Peng read the text very well. (complement with 得)

7. She made a lot of progress with her pronunciation.

8. In the beginning, he didn't speak Chinese clearly.

9. Do not laugh at other people.

10. I hope you will make a lot of progress with your Chinese.

11. Previously, she told me that her major was computers.

12. When I went to see her, she was writing a letter to her boyfriend. (. . . 的时候， . . . 正在 . . .)

Writing Practice

Write your friend a letter in Chinese telling him/her about your experience
learning Chinese.

Example:

My Chinese class is hard, but I think it is pretty interesting. My Chinese friend often helps me, and that is the reason my Chinese has improved rapidly. In addition to practicing speaking Chinese, I also play ball and go to movies with my friend. Both my friend and I are happy.

LESSON 9 ▲ Shopping
第九课 ▲ 买东西
Dì jiǔ kè ▲ *Mǎi dōngxi*

Part One

DIALOGUE I: BUYING CLOTHING

I. Listening Comprehension

A. Textbook Dialogue I (Multiple Choice)

(   ) 1. What color shirt does the customer want to buy?

      a. black   b. white   c. red   d. yellow

(   ) 2. What else does the customer want to buy besides the shirt?

      a. a hat   b. a pair of shoes

      c. a sweater   d. a pair of pants

(   ) 3. What size does the customer wear?

      a. small   b. medium   c. large   d. extra large

(   ) 4. How much does the customer need to pay altogether?

      a. between $20 and $30   b. between $30 and $40

      c. between $40 and $50   d. between $50 and $60

B. Workbook Narrative (Multiple Choice)

(   ) 1. What color does Wang Peng like?

      a. blue   b. brown   c. white   d. red

(   ) 2. Why does Wang Peng not like the shirt? Because of the:

      a. price   b. style   c. color   d. size

(   ) 3. What colors are the shirts that the salesperson says they have?

      a. white, blue, and brown   b. white, red, and brown

      c. red, blue, and white   d. white, red, and yellow

(   ) 4. When did Wang Peng buy the shirt?

      a. 5 days ago   b. 7 days ago   c. 10 days ago   d. 14 days ago

▼ ▼

II. Speaking Exercises

A. Answer the questions in Chinese based on Textbook Dialogue I.

1. What does the woman want to buy?

2. Is the woman very rich? How do you know?

3. Give the price for each item, and the total cost.

4. If the woman gives the salesperson $100, how much change should she receive?

B. You are in a department store, trying to buy a shirt and a pair of pants. Tell the salesperson what color and size you want.

C. Describe the four pictures below without looking at the textbook.

III. Reading Comprehension

A. Answer the questions about Textbook Dialogue I.

1. 李小姐买了一件什么颜色的衬衫?

2. 她买了一条多大的裤子？

3. 衬衫一件多少钱？ 裤子一条多少钱？

4. 售货员找了多少钱给李小姐？

B. Read the following passage and answer the questions. (True/False)

小高上个周末去买东西。他想买一件中号的红衬衫，可是中号衬衫都是白的，红衬衫都是大号的。售货员是一位很客气的小姐。她帮小高找了一件衬衫，不是红的，可是颜色也不错。那位售货员告诉他，这件衬衫三十九块九毛九。小高觉得太贵了一点儿，可是他觉得要是不买就对不起那位小姐，所以他买了那件衬衫。

Questions:

( ) 1. There were many choices in the store for Xiao Gao to select from.

( ) 2. The saleswoman was very helpful.

( ) 3. Last weekend Xiao Gao was looking for a white shirt.

( ) 4. Xiao Gao bought the shirt because he thought he shouldn't disappoint the saleswoman.

( ) 5. Xiao Gao wears a medium size shirt.

IV. Writing & Grammar Exercises

Grammar and Usage

Give Chinese characters for the following dollar amounts.

1. $5.12   _____
2. $18.50   _____
3. $70.05   _____
4. $99.99   _____
5. $100.60   _____

Translation

Translate the following sentences into Chinese, using the words or phrases in parentheses.

1. Would you like to watch TV or listen to music? （想，还是）

2. That large-size shirt is my older brother's, and this small-size one is mine. （的）

3. The yellow shirts are expensive, and the white ones are cheap. （Adj. + 的）

4. The medium red shirt is $8.95. Your change is one dollar.

5. The new words in Lesson Nine are not too many, and not too few, either.

6. A bottle of beer is $3.00 and a glass of cola is 75¢. (That's) $3.75 altogether.

▼ ▼

7. The salesperson asked what he would like to buy.

8. You pay here. It's $436.72 altogether.

9. What size do you wear? (多大)

Writing Practice

A. Write a shopping list in Chinese, including the names and prices of the items you want to purchase.

B. *Describe what you are wearing in Chinese. Don't forget to mention color and size.*

▼ ▼

Part Two

DIALOGUE II: EXCHANGING SHOES

I. Listening Comprehension

A. Textbook Dialogue II (True/False)

Quote the key sentence from the dialogue to support your answer.

(   ) 1. Why does the lady want to exchange the shoes?

     a. The shoes do not fit well.

     b. The shoes are damaged.

     c. She does not like the price.

     d. She does not like the color.

(   ) 2. What color does the lady prefer?

     a. black   b. white   c. brown   d. red

(   ) 3. In what way are the new pair of shoes like the old pair? They are:

     a. the same size.   b. the same color.

     c. the same price.   d. the same design.

B. Workbook Dialogue (True/False)

Quote the key sentence from the dialogue to support your answer.

(   ) 1. The man returned his shirt for a different one, because he didn't like the color.

(   ) 2. The man finally took a yellow shirt because he liked the color.

(   ) 3. All the large-size shirts in the store are yellow ones.

(   ) 4. A large-size shirt fits the man well.

II. Speaking Exercises

A. Answer the questions in Chinese based on Textbook Dialogue II.

1. Why did the woman want to return the shoes for a different pair?

2. Does the woman like black shoes? Explain.

3. What color of shoes did she finally accept? Why?

4. Did the woman pay any additional money for the new shoes? Explain.

B. You bought a shirt that is too large. Try to exchange it for a smaller one.

C. Describe the clothes you are wearing today.

III. Reading Comprehension

A. Answer the questions about Textbook Dialogue II.

1. 李小姐为什么想换鞋？

2. 李小姐想换什么颜色的鞋？

3. 李小姐换了鞋没有？ 她换了一双什么鞋？

B. Read the passage and answer the questions.

上星期六，小张买了一条裤子。她想买黑色的，可是只有黄的和红的，她买了一条红的。回家以后，觉得不太喜欢那条裤子的颜色，想明天下午去换一条别的颜色的裤子。

Questions:

1. 上星期六小张买了什么颜色的裤子？

2. 小张喜欢什么颜色的裤子？

3. 小张为什么不喜欢她的新裤子？

4. 明天下午小张要做什么？

C. Read the passage and answer the questions (True/False).

李太太很喜欢买东西，最喜欢买便宜的衣服。虽然她的衣服很多，可是都不太合适。李先生跟他太太不一样，不喜欢买东西，也不常买东西。李先生只买大小合适的衣服，所以，李先生的衣服虽然不多，可是都很合适。

Questions:

( ) 1. 李太太觉得买东西很有意思。

( ) 2. 李太太的衣服很多，也都很贵。

( ) 3. 李太太的衣服大小和颜色都很合适。

( ) 4. 李先生觉得买衣服没意思。

( ) 5. 李先生买了很多衣服。

( ) 6. 李先生的衣服不大也不小。

D. Find the clothing items corresponding to the descriptions below. Place the correct letter in the parentheses next to its description. [Note: This exercise contains supplementary vocabulary items.]

1. 短裤（ ）   2. 长裤（ ）   3. 大衣（ ）

4. 帽子（ ）   5. 袜子（ ）   6. 裙子（ ）

7. T-恤衫（ ）   8. 西装（ ）   9. 夹克（ ）

10. 外套（ ）   11. 毛衣（ ）

IV. Writing & Grammar Exercises

Grammar and Usage

A. Fill in each of the blanks with an appropriate measure word.

件，条，双，本，瓶，位，节，封，篇，杯

1. 一 ＿＿＿＿ 鞋   2. 一 ＿＿＿＿ 衬衫

3. 两 ＿＿＿＿ 裤子   4. 三 ＿＿＿＿ 课

5. 一 ＿＿＿＿ 先生   6. 一 ＿＿＿＿ 书

▼ ▼

7. 一 _____ 日记   8. 两 _____ 信

9. 一 _____ 可乐   10. 一 _____ 茶

B. Complete the following sentences.

1. 这条裤子虽然颜色不太好，_____。

   (inexpensive)

2. 我虽然喜欢看电影，_____。 (don't

   have time)

3. _____ (very difficult), 可是我很喜欢学。

4. 虽然他上个月才开始学中文，_____

   _____。 (speaks quite well)

5. _____ (I don't write well)，可是我很喜欢

   写汉字。

C. Following the model, complete the following sentences using the pattern "A 跟 B 一样 + Adj."

   Example: 我的衬衫<u>跟我哥哥的衬衫一样贵</u>。
            （贵）

1. 这双鞋_____。（大）

2. 学英文_____。（有意思）

3. 我的裤子的颜色_____。（漂亮）

4. 你说中文_____。（快）

5. 第七课的功课_____。（难）

6. 学校餐厅的饭_____。（好吃）

D. Complete the following dialogue.

售货员：_____?

李小姐：我想买一条裤子。

售货员：_____?

李小姐：大号的。

售货员：这条太大了，你可以换_____

　　　　_____。

李小姐：中号的很合适。

售货员：_____?

李小姐：还要买一双鞋。

售货员：_____?

▼▼▼

李小姐：黄的。

售货员：一条裤子十九块，一双鞋十五

块，一共 _____。

李小姐：_____。

售货员：找您六十六块。

Translation

Translate the following sentences into Chinese, using the words or phrases in parentheses.

1. Do you want to buy a pair of black shoes or a pair of yellow ones?
（要，还是）

2. This pair of pants is just as expensive as that pair.

3. The color of your shirt is the same as mine.

4. Although this pair of shoes fits me well, I don't like the color. （虽然）

5. The brown shoes are not too expensive, but not too cheap, either.

6. You don't need to give me the change.

Writing Practice

Translate the following passage into Chinese.

Yesterday I bought a yellow shirt and a pair of black pants. The pants are very expensive, but the color is very nice and the size is right. Although the shirt is very pretty and also very cheap, it's too small. Tomorrow I'll exchange it for a large shirt.

LESSON 10 ▲ Talking about the Weather
第十课 ▲ 谈天气
Dì shí kè ▲ *Tán tiānqì*

Part One

DIALOGUE I: THE WEATHER IS GETTING BETTER

I. Listening Comprehension

A. Textbook Dialogue I (True/False)

Quote the key sentence from the dialogue to support your answer.

(T) 1. It rained yesterday. (不下雨了)

(T) 2. The weather today is better than yesterday. (今天天气比昨天好。)

(T) 3. It will be warmer tomorrow than today. (不但不会下雨，而且会暖和一点儿)

(F) 4. Miss Li will go to see the red leaves tomorrow. 李小姐今天早上跟王先生去上海了。

(F) 5. Mr. Wang went to Shanghai by himself.

(T) 6. The woman suggests that the man stay home tomorrow. 你在家看录像吧。

B. Workbook Dialogue I (Multiple Choice)

(C) 1. What season is it now?

    a. spring   b. summer   c. autumn   d. winter

(   ) 2. Where was the woman this afternoon?

    a. in the classroom   b. in the park

    c. in the shopping mall   d. in the office

(D) 3. How will the weather be tomorrow?

    a. rainy   b. hot   c. sunny   d. warm

(B) 4. The man got the information on the weather from:

    a. the TV.   b. the newspaper.

    c. his friend.   d. the radio.

II. Speaking Exercises

A. Answer the questions in Chinese based on Textbook Dialogue I.

    1. What did the weather forecast say about the weather tomorrow?

    2. Was the man excited about the forecast of tomorrow's weather? Why?

    3. Where will Miss Li most likely be tomorrow?

    4. What did the woman suggest the man do tomorrow?

B. Compare two objects (books, pieces of clothing items, etc.) or two people (family members, friends, etc.).

C. Compare the two languages, Chinese and English.

III. Reading Comprehension

A. Answer the questions about Textbook Dialogue I.

1. 今天天气怎么样？

2. 高先生明天想做什么事？

3. 天气预报说明天的天气怎么样？

4. 高先生跟李小姐明天会去看红叶吗？为什么？

B. Read the following passage and answer the questions. (True/False)

星期五下午王朋约了李友星期天一起去公园看红叶。可是星期六报上的天气预报说，星期天会下雨。王朋就给李友打了一个电话，告诉她星期天不去公园了。星期天上午王朋请李友来他的宿舍看录像，可是星期天的天气很好，不但没下雨，而且很暖和。王朋说："以后报上说会下雨，我们就可以去公园看红叶。报上说天气很好，我们就只能在家看录像了。"

Questions:

(   ) 1. The story took place in summer.

(   ) 2. They had to change their plan for Sunday because of the weather forecast.

(   ) 3. Wang Peng learned the weather forecast from the TV.

(   ) 4. Wang Peng was glad that he and Li You were not out on Sunday.

(   ) 5. Wang Peng thinks that the weather forecast is very reliable.

IV. Writing & Grammar Exercises

Grammar and Usage

A. Following the model, make sentences using the structure "不但...而且...".

Example: 漂亮 / 便宜

→ 这件衬衫不但很漂亮，而且很便宜。

1. 喜欢听音乐/喜欢看录像：

2. 常常下雨/冷：

3. 贵/颜色不好：

4. 不便宜/不合适：

5. 想去买东西/想去看红叶：

B. Complete the sentences and expand the dialogue.

A: 小谢，明天是星期六，我们去公园看红叶，

_____？

B: 好啊，可是我听天气预报说

_____。

A: 那我们星期天再去吧。

▼▼▼

B: 可是下个星期天的天气

_____ 。

A: 那怎么办呢？

B: _____ 。

Translation

Translate the following sentences into Chinese, using the words or phrases in parentheses.

1. We can not only speak Chinese but also write letters in Chinese. （不但...而且...）

2. English is difficult, but Japanese is more difficult. （更）

3. The weather forecast in the newspaper says that the weather will be better next week. （会）

4. Eating Chinese food is more convenient than eating American food.
（比）

5. The black shoes are more expensive than the red ones. （比）

6. I would like to make a date with Miss Li to go to the park to see the red leaves.

7. Watching a video is cheaper than going to the movies.

Writing Practice

Write a paragraph comparing two things or people. Be sure to use these expressions: 不但...而且..., *and* 比.

▼▼

Part Two

DIALOGUE: COMPLAINING ABOUT THE WEATHER

I. Listening Comprehension

A. Textbook Dialogue II (True/False)

Quote the key sentence from the dialogue to support your answer.

(   ) 1. It has been raining often recently.

(   ) 2. The weather will be better next week.

(   ) 3. This weekend is not a good time to go out, for it is going to be cold and wet.

(   ) 4. It will be hotter in two months.

(   ) 5. Little Ye is in Taiwan for a visit.

(   ) 6. The best time to visit Taiwan is in the spring.

B. Workbook Dialogue II (True/False)

Quote the key sentence from the dialogue to support your answer.

(   ) 1. Wang Peng had an outing with Li You today.

(   ) 2. Wang Peng does not like the weather because it started to rain in the morning.

(   ) 3. The weather forecast says that the weather will be somewhat better tomorrow.

(   ) 4. Tomorrow Wang Peng will be preparing his lessons for Monday.

(   ) 5. Wang Peng believes that next Saturday it will be even cooler than tomorrow.

(   ) 6. The dialogue most likely occurred on a Sunday.

II. Speaking Exercises

A. Answer the questions in Chinese based on Textbook Dialogue II.

1. What did the newspaper say about the weather this week and next week?

2. Why couldn't they go out to have fun this weekend?

3. Describe Taiwan's weather.

4. Why is Little Xia not very familiar with the weather in Taiwan?

▼▼

B. *Describe the climate of your hometown.*

C. *Compare the weather of your hometown with the weather of another place.*

III. Reading Comprehension

A. *Answer the questions about Textbook Dialogue II.*

1. 小夏怎么知道这个星期的天气都不好？

2. 台北夏天的天气很舒服，对不对？

3. 小叶住 (zhù: to live) 在哪儿？

4. 台湾什么时候天气最好？

B. *Read the passage and answer the questions. (True/False)*

黄先生以前住 (zhù: to live) 在台中，台中的天气很好，常常不冷不热，很舒服。黄先生现在在台北工作。台北的冬天天气很糟糕，不但很冷，而且常常下雨。他看报上的天气预报说这个周末台北会下雨，可是台中的天气很好，他想约夏小姐星期天到台中去玩。

Questions:

( ) 1. 黄先生现在不住在台中了。

( ) 2. 台中的天气很不错。

( ) 3. 台北的冬天虽然常常下雨，可是很暖和。

( ) 4. 这个周末台北的天气比台中好。

( ) 5. 黄先生听朋友说这个周末台北会下雨。

( ) 6. 夏小姐住在台中。

C. Read the passage and answer the questions. (True/False)

[Note: See the supplementary vocabulary list for the new words.]

叶小姐一个人在加拿大的温哥华工作，她的爸爸妈妈住在香港。叶小姐常常去看她的爸爸妈妈，可是她不喜欢夏天回香港，因为香港的夏天又闷又热。叶小姐想请她爸爸妈妈到温哥华来住。可是她的爸爸妈妈已经习惯了香港的天气，而且他们在加拿大没有朋友，所以他们觉得住在那儿没有意思。

Questions:

( ) 1. 叶小姐的爸爸妈妈常常来加拿大。

( ) 2. 叶小姐常常在夏天回香港。

( ) 3. 叶小姐的爸爸妈妈不觉得香港的夏天太热。

( ) 4. 叶小姐的爸爸妈妈在温哥华没有朋友。

( ) 5. 叶小姐觉得温哥华夏天的天气比香港好。

( ) 6. 叶小姐的爸爸妈妈觉得住在香港比住在温哥华有意思。

D. Read the following dialogue and answer the questions. (True/False)

（老王和老李打电话聊天。）

老王：要是我下个月工作不忙，我想去台北玩儿。

老李：你最好秋天来，下个月这儿天气太热了。九月以后会凉快一点儿。

老王：台北的冬天怎么样？

老李：冬天？冬天比夏天更糟糕，不但冷，而且常常下雨。

老王：是吗？那我们这儿的天气比你们那儿好，不冷也不热。

老李：真的啊？那太舒服了！

Questions:

( ) 1. Most likely the telephone conversation took place in September.

( ) 2. Lao Li lives in Taipei.

( ) 3. According to Lao Li, the best season to visit Taipei is autumn.

( ) 4. In comparison with summer, winter in Taipei is a little better.

( ) 5. Winter in Taipei is dry, not cold.

IV. Writing & Grammar Exercises

Grammar and Usage

A. Choose the appropriate adverbs to fill in the blanks. （真，太，又，再，更，很）

1. 今天的天气 _____ 热了。

2. 这个录像 _____ 好看，我要 _____ 看一次。

3. 这件衣服 _____ 便宜 _____ 好看。

4. 上个星期的天气不好，这个星期的天气 _____ 糟糕。

5. 我觉得写中国字 _____ 有意思。

6. 他喜欢看电视，但是他 _____ 喜欢打球。

7. 他昨天给他弟弟打了一个电话，今天 _____ 给他打了一个电话。

8. 这儿 _____ 有意思，我们下个月 _____ 来一次，好吗？

9. 昨天晚上他不在家，我想他 _____ 去看电影了。

10. 第五课的生词 _____ 多，可是第六课的生词 _____ 多。

B. Rewrite the sentences in each group into one sentence that expresses a comparison with the word 比.

Example: 昨天的天气热。今天的天气不太热。

→ 今天的天气比昨天凉快。

or: 昨天的天气比今天热。

1. 他这个星期很忙。他上个星期不太忙。

2. 中文很难，日文更难。

3. 这本书贵。那本书更贵。

4. 台湾的春天不舒服，秋天舒服。

5. 这儿的天气很暖和。那儿的天气更暖和。

C. Write a sentence for each of the situations given below.

Example: Today's temperatures: Shanghai, ninety-five degrees; Beijing, seventy-five degrees.

→ 今天上海比北京热。

or: 今天北京比上海凉快。

1. Today's temperatures: Hong Kong, ninety degrees; Shanghai, eighty-five degrees.

2. Prices for the shirts: yellow ones, $16 each; white ones, $18 each.

3. Mr. Wang is 5'8"; Mr. Wang's son is 6'2."

4. Little Bai has five books; Little Li has eight books.

5. Chinese is hard; Japanese is harder.

6. Lawyer Zhang is very polite; Lawyer Gao is not too polite.

7. The yellow shirt is not that pretty; the red shirt is very pretty.

8. Beer is expensive; cola is not that expensive.

9. Watching TV is not very interesting; going to the movies is really fun.

10. My father's office is big; my mother's office is not that big.

Translation

Translate the following sentences into Chinese, using the words or phrases in parentheses.

1. This shirt is both nice and cheap. (又 . . . 又 . . .)

2. Summer in Taiwan is indeed awful! It is both hot and humid. (又 . . . 又 . . .)

3. This shirt is not only very expensive, but also very ugly. (不但 . . . 而且 . . .)

4. Li You wrote a letter to her mother last week. She wrote her another letter this week. (select 又 or 再)

5. I called her yesterday, but she wasn't home. I will call her again today. (select 又 or 再)

6. He went to a movie again last night. (select 又 or 再)

7. It was very hot yesterday, but it is even hotter today. (更)

8. I didn't know how to speak Chinese before, but now I do. (了)

9. The weather is not good today. I'm not going to the park to see the red leaves. (不 … 了)

10. She was very busy yesterday, but she is no longer busy today. (不 … 了)

11. What a mess! It's raining again. I'm not going out any more. (糟糕)

12. Next time you had better go to Taipei in the fall. Autumn in Taiwan is very comfortable.

13. The summer here is warm, but not hot.

Writing Practice

A. Describe today's weather.

B. Give the Chinese version of the passage below.

> I work in Taipei, but both my older brother and older sister are in Shanghai. The weather in Shanghai is different from that in Taipei. The summer in Taipei is somewhat cooler than Shanghai. Although the winter in Shanghai is colder than Taipei, it is a bit more comfortable there. I'd like to go to Shanghai to see my brother and sister this fall.

LESSON 11 ▲ Transportation

第十一课 ▲ 交通

Dì shíyī kè ▲ *Jiāotōng*

Part One

DIALOGUE: GOING HOME FOR THE WINTER VACATION

I. Listening Comprehension

A. Textbook Dialogue (True/False)

Quote the key sentence from the dialogue to support your answer.

( ) 1. Li You is leaving home for school on the twenty-first.

( ) 2. Li You should reach the airport no later than 8:00 p.m.

( ) 3. Li You decided not to take a taxi because she thought it was too expensive.

( ) 4. Li You didn't know how to get to the airport by subway.

( ) 5. In order to get to the airport, Li You can take the subway first, then the bus.

( ) 6. Li You finally agreed to go to the airport in Wang Peng's car.

B. Workbook Dialogue I (True/False)

Quote the key sentence from the dialogue to support your answer.

( ) 1. The woman has decided to go home for the summer.

( ) 2. The man invites the woman to visit his home.

( ) 3. The man and the woman will drive to the man's home together.

( ) 4. Airline tickets are not expensive now.

II. Speaking Exercises

A. Answer the questions in Chinese based on the Textbook Dialogue.

1. What will Li You do for the winter vacation?

2. Has Li You made any travel plans for her winter vacation? Explain.

3. Explain how to get to the airport from the school by bus and subway.

4. Will Li You go to the airport by taxi? Why?

B. *You need to buy airplane tickets for your winter vacation. Call your travel agent and reserve a ticket for December 22. Tell your travel agent that you prefer a morning flight.*

C. *What is the best way to get to the airport from your home? Are there any other alternatives?*

III. Reading Comprehension

A. *Answer the questions about the Textbook Dialogue.*

1. 李友的飞机票是哪天的？

2. 李友坐几点的飞机？

3. 要是李友坐地铁或者公共汽车，怎么走？

4. 为什么李友说"太麻烦了"?

5. 为什么王朋不要李友坐出租汽车?

6. 李友最后怎么去机场?

B. Read the following note and answer the questions. (True/False)

小李:

　　请你明天到我家来吃晚饭，因为明天是我的生日。到我家来你可以坐四号公共汽车，也可以坐地铁，都很方便。坐公共汽车慢，可是不用换车。坐地铁快，但是得换车，先坐红线，坐三站，然后换蓝线，坐两站下车就到了。希望你能来！明天见。

　　　　　　　　　　小白

　　　　　　　　　　二月十七日下午三点

Questions:

( ) 1. 小李要请小白吃晚饭。

( ) 2. 坐地铁去小白家比坐公共汽车快。

( ) 3. 坐地铁或者坐公共汽车都得换车。

( ) 4. 小白的生日是二月八号。

( ) 5. 坐地铁去小白家一共要坐五站，还得
换车。

IV. Writing & Grammar Exercises

Grammar and Usage

A. Change the following sentences so that they reflect the "topic-comment" structure.

Example: 她喜欢那件衬衫吗？

→ 那件衬衫她很喜欢 。

1. 你复习昨天的语法了吗？

2. 你买飞机票了吗？

3. 你们都很喜欢喝中国茶吗？

4. 你不习惯这儿的天气吗？

B. Complete the following sentences with "还是 . . . 吧."

1. 今天的天气真不好，别出去了，_____
_____。(看电视)

2. 这件衣服太贵，那件虽然颜色不好，可是
很便宜。我 _____
_____。（买）

3.A: 我们今天晚上吃中国饭还是吃美国饭？

  B: _____。

4.A: 明天又有中国电影，又有音乐会，你说
我们去哪儿？

  B: _____。

C. Write sentences using "先 . . . 再 . . . ," based on the information given below.
Example: 下课以后，他要去图书馆。

→他先上课，再去图书馆。

1. 王朋八点吃早饭，九点上电脑课。

2. 坐公共汽车以前，你得坐地铁。

3. 我十月五日去日本，十一月六日去英国。

4. 他吃晚饭以后去看电影。

5. 李友下午两点去图书馆，四点钟去打球。

D. Fill in the blanks with 或者 *or* 还是.

1. 他是中国人＿＿＿＿美国人？

2. 到你家去，坐地铁方便 ＿＿＿＿坐公共汽车方便？

3. 你想买红色的，黄色的， ＿＿＿＿绿色的？

4. 今天晚上我想在家看书 ＿＿＿＿看电视。

5. 我想要一杯咖啡 ＿＿＿＿一瓶可乐。

Translation

Translate the following sentences into Chinese, using the words or phrases in parentheses.

1. It is raining. You had better stay home and watch videos. (还是 . . . 吧)

2. *A:* Should I take the bus or the subway to go to the airport?

B: You can go to the airport either by bus or by subway.

3. Could you give me a ride to the airport tomorrow? (开车)

4. I have seen <u>that Chinese movie</u>. (topic-comment)

5. Let's learn the pronunciation before we learn the characters. (先 . . . 再 . . .)

6. First, you take the bus, then change to the subway. Finally you have to take a taxi. (先 . . . 再 . . . ， 最后 . . .)

7. It's too much trouble to write him a letter. Let's call him instead. (还是)

8. You can go to the airport by subway. First, you take the green line, and then you change to the blue line.

9. We will meet at the bus stop at 6:00 p.m.

10. Do you know where to get off?

Writing Practice

Describe in detail how to get to the airport from your school.

Part Two

A LETTER: THANKING SOMEONE FOR A RIDE

I. Listening Comprehension

A. A Letter (True/False)

Quote the key sentence from the dialogue to support your answer.

(   ) 1. Wang Peng gave Li You a ride to the airport.

(   ) 2. Li You cannot drive.

(   ) 3. There is bus service but no subway in Li You's hometown.

(   ) 4. Li You was busy visiting old friends.

(   ) 5. Li You felt that everybody drove too slowly.

(   ) 6. Li You very much enjoyed driving on the highway.

B. Workbook Dialogue II

(   ) 1. The woman knew how to get to Little Gao's home.

(   ) 2. To get to Little Gao's home by subway, one must first take the red line, then change to the blue line.

(   ) 3. The woman decides to go to Little Gao's home by bus.

(   ) 4. There is a bus stop in front of Little Gao's house.

C. Workbook Dialogue III

(   ) 1. Old Zhang doesn't know how to drive.

(   ) 2. There is a highway going to the airport.

(   ) 3. Old Zhang will go to the airport with the woman.

(   ) 4. The woman will go to the airport by taxi.

II. Speaking Exercises

A. Answer the questions in Chinese based on A Letter: Thanking Someone for a Ride.

1. How do you express New Year greetings in Chinese?

2. Why did Li You thank Wang Peng?

3. What has Li You been doing for the past few days?

4. Is Li You a good driver? Please explain.

B. Call your friend and thank him/her for the ride to the airport. Tell him/her what you have been doing since you returned home, and wish your friend a happy New Year.

C. Explain how to get to the airport from your friend's house by referring to the picture below.

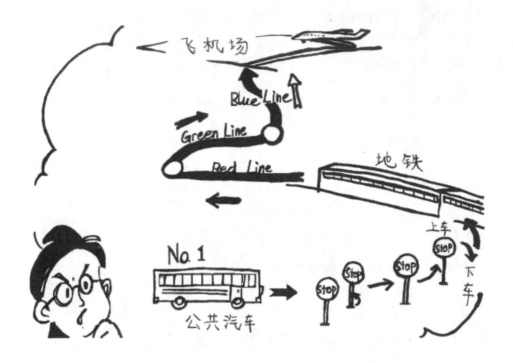

III. Reading Comprehension

A. Answer the questions about A Letter: Thanking Someone for a Ride.

1. 为什么李友觉得不好意思?

2. 李友回家以后，每天都做什么?

3. 为什么李友开车很紧张?

4. 为什么李友开车很紧张，可是还是得自己开车？

B. Read the following diary entry and answer the questions. (True/False)

李友的一篇日记

今天是我第一次在高速公路上开车。我开车去小王家找他去打球。高速公路上的汽车不但多，而且都开得很快。因为我很紧张，所以迷路 (mílù: to lose one's way) 了。我的车上有电话。就给小王打电话，小王告诉我怎么走。因为我迷路了，所以很晚才到小王家。

Questions:

( ) 1. 李友常常在高速公路上开车。

( ) 2. 高速公路上的汽车都开得很快。

( ) 3. 李友开车的时候不紧张。

( ) 4. 李友可以在她的车上打电话。

( ) 5. 今天的天气很不好，所以李友迷路了。

( ) 6. 因为李友迷路了，所以小王开车来帮忙。

( ) 7. 李友去小王家，因为小王请她吃晚饭。

C. Read the following note and answer the questions. (True/False)

张英，你好。我是小白。我昨天才知道你这个星期六要坐飞机去中国。你告诉王朋了，可是怎么没告诉我呢？你别坐公共汽车去机场。坐公共汽车不但不舒服，而且很慢。你得坐五站，还要换地铁，太麻烦了。我可以开车送你到机场去。我们走高速公路，很快就可以到机场。我开车开得很好，因为我常常在高速公路上开车。你回学校以后给我打个电话，好吗？要是你的飞机票已经买好了，我想知道你的飞机是几点钟的。好，再见。

Questions:

( ) 1. Zhang Ying will go to China with Xiao Bai.

( ) 2. Wang Peng knows that Zhang Ying is going to China.

( ) 3. According to Xiao Bai, the public transportation to the airport is not convenient.

( ) 4. Xiao Bai considers himself a good driver.

( ) 5. Xiao Bai does not know Zhang Ying's flight schedule.

D. Read the following passage and answer the questions. (True/False)

小白今天开车送张英去机场。高速公路上汽车很多，而且开得都很快，小白很紧张，所以走错了。张英的飞机是两点半的，可是他们三点钟才到机场。机场的人告诉张英，她只能坐明天的飞机了。小白

很不好意思。他说："明天我再开车送你
吧。"可是张英说："谢谢。你还是在家看
看录像吧。我明天可以坐出租汽车。"

Questions:

( ) 1. Xiao Bai is a very experienced driver.

( ) 2. The traffic on the highway was light, but people drove fast.

( ) 3. Xiao Bai took the wrong way because he was nervous.

( ) 4. When they arrived at the airport, the airplane had left.

( ) 5. There were later flights today, but Zhang Ying preferred to wait till tomorrow.

( ) 6. Most likely Zhang Ying will not go to the airport with Xiao Bai tomorrow.

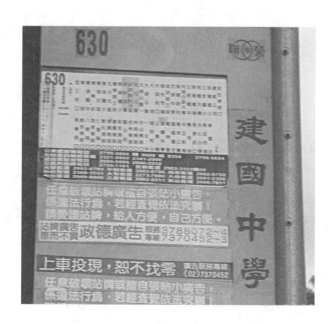

E. Read the following passage and answer the questions.

每年的中国新年小孩都很高兴，因为他们
不但可以穿新衣，新鞋，而且爸爸妈妈还
会给他们钱。不过，小夏告诉我她不喜欢
中国新年，因为她已经三十岁，有先生

了。除了别人不能给她钱以外，她还得给别人钱。小夏又说新年的时候公共汽车很少，她自己也没有车，所以出去玩也不方便。她觉得中国新年太没意思了。

Questions:

1. What are the two things during Chinese New Year that make children so happy? Explain in detail.

2. What are the two things during Chinese New Year that make Xiao Xia unhappy? Explain in detail.

3. Is Xiao Xia male or female? How do you know?

IV. Writing & Grammar Exercises

Grammar and Usage

A. Rewrite the following sentences with 每...都 *(měi...dōu).*

    Example: 他晚上看电视。

        →他每天晚上都看电视。

1. 小高写的字都很好看。

2. 她早上走高速公路。

3. 考试的时候学生很紧张。

4. 小白寒假坐飞机回家。

5. 我的朋友会开车。

Translation

Translate the following sentences into Chinese, using the words or phrases in parentheses.

1. I listen to the tapes every morning. （每...都）

2. I feel really bad that I let you spend so much money.

3. For the past few days, driving on the highway every day has made me rather nervous.

4. Little Bai has no friends. So, he wished himself a Happy New Year.

Writing Practice

A. Describe your experiences driving or traveling on the highway.

B. Translate the following passage into Chinese.

Winter vacation starts next week. During winter vacation I will go home to see my mom and dad. My dad bought me a plane ticket. (会) My mom called me yesterday. She told me that she had bought me three new shirts—a blue one, a red one, and a green one. Dad will drive to the airport, and my younger brother will go with him. I talked to Mom in Chinese. (用 . . . V . . .) She said that my Chinese had improved. I was very happy.